Contents

Dedication

This report is dedicated to
William T. Gruhn
whose pioneering work in the articulation
of the functions of middle level
education provided the foundation
of this study.

—*The NASSP Council on Middle Level Education*

Acknowledgments

The many educators who contributed to this research project deserve much gratitude: the 141 observers who each gave a full day of their time to secure the basic data; the 21 general analysts and 24 comparative analysts who studied, summarized, and analyzed packets of studies; and Joel Milgram, University of Cincinnati, who graciously consented to prepare the chapter on the ninth grader.

In addition, the interest, support, and direct assistance of the NASSP Middle Level Committee and Council is appreciated. George Melton, deputy executive director, worked diligently to launch and carry out this project. Our distinguished colleagues, Conrad Toepfer and Alfred Arth, were a constant source of help and insight. James Keefe, NASSP director of research, provided valuable advice and assistance. Patricia Rodgers and Peggy Bareswilt deserve special thanks for their assistance in manuscript preparation.

A very special thank you is also extended to Kathleen Thurlow, who handled all the correspondence, records, reproduction of copies, and administrative details. Her personal interest in the project was a major factor in ensuring its successful completion.

Finally, appreciation is extended to Tom Koerner, director of publications, and Carol Bruce, assistant director, who edited the manuscript and directed its publication.

While all of the above should be given credit for their important contributions, the writers, who assumed responsibility for reviewing all the materials and preparing this written report, accept responsibility for any deficiencies that may exist.

John H. Lounsbury
J. Howard Johnston

CHAPTER 1

The Ninth Grade Study: Why and How

Prevailing educational wisdom and, increasingly, common practice would seem to support the generalization that the ninth grade belongs in the high school. A clear shift in school organizational patterns has been taking place during the past 20 years. While most of the attention during this period has been on establishing middle level schools, consisting primarily of grades 6 through 8, a concomitant occurrence has been the return of the ninth grade to the high school from whence it came when junior high schools were organized.

The justifications for establishing 6-8 middle schools were both educational and administrative. They ranged from the need to accommodate court ordered desegregation and declining enrollments to a recognition of the increased maturity of today's early adolescents and a genuine desire to meet their needs more adequately with a distinctive educational program. Also inherent in the reorganization thrust was the belief that the academic needs of the ninth grader would be better served in the upper unit, where more specialized teachers, enriched electives, and planned sequences would be available.

During the last two decades, nearly all the research efforts and expressions of professional opinion were centered on the middle school. Although no clear answer concerning its efficacy has emerged, it has been a much discussed and debated topic.

Yet, all the while this shift of many ninth grades was occurring, hundreds of other ninth grades have remained, and will undoubtedly remain for years to come, as inherent parts of well established, widely supported, and very effective junior high schools.

So how goes the ninth grade? Has it been well served when shifted back to the high school? Are ninth grade programs more effective when they are located in the upper unit rather than in a junior high school? Have high schools adequately accommodated ninth graders, or do established junior high schools serve their needs better? Do ninth grade programs, wherever they are located, reflect what we know about the nature and needs of 14 and 15-year-old youngsters?

The question "How fares the ninth grade?" is, then, very pertinent. Educators currently know relatively little about the ninth grade as an entity. It is, in many respects, a forgotten grade. And, in the eyes of many, it is an unwanted grade.

In the first decades of the reorganization movement, high school administrators seemed quite willing to give up their ninth grades to newly organized junior high schools. Early junior high schools, as would be expected, expressed belief in the validity of the 7-9 arrangement. As late as 1966, educators surveyed by Gruhn (1967) supported the 7-9 organization as the one in which a superior academic program could be developed.

1

But the proper place of the ninth grade had been questioned by many for more than a decade. James B. Conant (1960), in his *Recommendations for Education in the Junior High School Years,* concluded that, "There is no consensus whatever among experienced educators as to the place of grade nine in the organizational framework. Should it be the top grade in a three year junior high school or the bottom grade in a four year senior high school? I know of similar communities which recently arrived at opposite conclusions." (P. 11.)

As the middle school movement gained momentum, many intermediate level administrators openly expressed relief when the ninth grade was moved back to the upper unit. The ninth grade is, then, the focus of an old and continuing issue. But should the location of the ninth grade, in and of itself, be an issue at all? Will a review of the status of ninth grade programs reveal truths that will guide educational decisions about the preferred placement or about improvements needed irrespective of placement?

Clearly, it is time to take a serious look at the ninth grade. As a means of doing this, the research project reported herein was developed and carried out under the auspices of the NASSP Middle Level Committee and Council. The project sought to answer three questions:

1. What is the school day for the individual ninth grader really like?
2. Is the educational program being provided ninth graders compatible with the nature and needs of youth at this age level?
3. Does the educational program provided in the ninth grade vary depending on the type of organizational unit in which the grade is housed?

To seek answers to these questions a naturalistic or quasi-ethnographic approach was selected as the means of gathering data. So often in education we describe curriculum in terms of courses of study or content to be covered. But, as the late Kimbell Wiles reminded us, "The real curriculum is the one the pupil experiences. Actually, the expectations of curriculum designers may be illusions and the teacher's guides and syllabi mere paper representations of hollow hopes." (Lounsbury and Marani, 1964, p.v.)

And so it is. These words state succinctly and fairly a reality we all too seldom acknowledge. It is not really fair to assess a school's program by examining the course of study or even by watching the teacher's performance. What counts is what the individual pupil experiences—and what a single pupil experiences is not necessarily what the teacher is teaching or what the class in general is experiencing.

This point of view led the Council to select the Shadow Study technique, which has proven effective in sociological and educational studies, including two earlier studies of middle level grades. The procedure involves the observing (or shadowing) of randomly selected students during a particular day in school. Observers record the students' behavior and learning environment at stated intervals throughout the entire school day. The studies, taken together, present a picture of education from the consumer's standpoint. (Appendix A provides additional details on the Shadow Study technique along with some observer's reactions to it.)

Volunteers to serve as observers were solicited through announcements in the *NASSP NewsLeader* and contacts at the 1983 NASSP Convention in Las Vegas. These individuals, largely members of NASSP, were asked to conduct a shadow study on March 7, 1984. (See Appendix B for list of observers, directions, and forms.)

One hundred forty-one volunteers completed the assignment. They spent March 7, 1984, shadowing a ninth grade student and recording that student's behavior and the educational environment in five to seven-minute intervals. At the close of the day, the student was interviewed. The observers also provided their own summaries of the day and their reactions. A limited amount of general information on the ninth grade program and the school was also secured.

2

Reports on the school day of ninth graders were received from 45 junior high schools, 71 high schools (9-12), and 25 junior-senior high schools. Forty-eight states and the District of Columbia were represented in the sample. (See Appendix C for list of schools.) These 141 shadow studies constitute the data base for the study.

A carefully designed and systematic process was employed to analyze the raw data. Twenty-one general analysts were selected: seven principals, seven teachers, and seven college professors, one of each from each of the seven NASSP regions. (Names of the general analysts are given in Appendix D.)

Each analyst received a set of 20 randomly selected studies, with identifying data removed, to read, react to, and summarize. Guidelines for directing the analysis and preparing the report were provided (See Appendix D-1.) Each individual study was read and analyzed by a teacher, a principal, and a college professor.

A different procedure was instituted to provide for a comparison between the three school types. Another group of analysts was established (Appendix E). Each of the 24 comparative analysts received a random group of 10 or 11 shadow studies with identifying data removed. This resulted in each study being evaluated by two different educators. Using a specifically designed checklist, individual studies were scored on the degree to which certain program conditions seemed to prevail in the shadow study reports. When returned, these coded checksheets were tabulated according to school type.

The results made it possible to see if there were differences between the way ninth graders were being educated when they were housed in a junior high school as opposed to a junior-senior high school or a four year high school. Additional details on the comparative analysis are included in chapter four.

Several limitations and conditions should be stated. First, the schools included in the study did not constitute a true random sample. They were not selected on the basis of any predetermined critera. They were simply the schools that were readily available to the volunteer observers.

Since the observers were active NASSP members, they may have used schools which would be somewhat above average in professional leadership and program. Second, all studies returned were analyzed, although some were incomplete or partially illegible. Third, the number of samples in the three school types varied, though they approximated the sizes of the populations.

Fourth, while observers were directed to choose a student in a random manner, it was obvious that the sample included considerably more above-average students than would be the case in a truly random sample. This might result in a composite picture that was more positive than would otherwise be the case. Fifth, observers differed in their levels of skill and perceptiveness and in the degree to which their reports combined objective and subjective comments. Finally, some observers were principals conducting the shadow study in their own school.

Whatever limitations may exist, the shadow studies themselves, the observers' summaries and reactions, and the extensive analyst's reports comprise a vast and powerful body of data. By reading the studies, one can vicariously visit some 900 classrooms, become privy to what 141 ninth grade students actually did in school one day and what they think about their schools, and ponder the summaries and opinions of 45 teachers, principals, and teacher educators.

One is hesitant to draw firm generalizations and to state definite conclusions, for the reports provide considerable evidence in support of almost any responsible position. Yet, the amazing consistency of the analysts' reactions stands out forcefully. Although there are few generalizations that can be made with completely universal support from the data,

3

those that are made are striking for the frequency with which they were advanced by the observers and analysts alike.

The writers believe almost anyone who studied these data would reach similar conclusions. It should also be noted that no real differences could be detected in the kinds of opinions expressed and conclusions reached by teachers, by principals, or by college professors. The near unanimity among and between the analysts regardless of position, certainly gives further strength and credence to the generalizations that emerge from these data.

While the limitations of ethnographic research are recognized, the danger of overgeneralization is noted, and the lack of scientific randomness in the sample is readily acknowledged, the force of these data, the degree of internal consistency between analysts, and the strong impressions of reality that arise simply cannot be put aside in the name of scientific accuracy.

There is, in our judgment, a validity to the composite picture painted which, to ignore, would be perilous indeed. We are convinced that these studies, in toto, do present a portrait of the ninth grade, both in the range of quality and in the generalized medium, that is both fair and correct and can serve as a basis for launching both improvement efforts and additional research.

The second chapter in the report consists of an overview of the nature of ninth graders. Readers are urged to peruse this chapter first. Curriculum and related decisions should, after all, be made in light of human growth and development, and the criteria for judging a program's adequacy, for the most part, should evolve from this foundation.

The third chapter summarizes the findings of the study relative to the nature of the ninth grader's day. It is based primarily on the reports of the general analysts and includes supportive notations drawn from both the analyst's reports and the observer's reactions. A section reporting on the results of the student interviews is also included in this chapter.

Chapter four presents the findings of the comparative analysis as well as some basic organizational and schoolwide data which relate to differences in the programs provided in junior high schools, comprehensive junior-senior high schools, and four-year high schools.

The fifth chapter is composed of six complete shadow studies. These studies were selected as representative of the type and range of the 141 studies. By studying these unaltered reports, readers will sample the data and be better able to understand and interpret the conclusions drawn. In fact, there is merit in reading these studies after reading chapter two and before delving into the other chapters.

As a supplement to these studies, 15 observer reactions are also included in this chapter. These perceptive analyses will further the reader's understanding of the data.

The last chapter presents the conclusions growing out of the project, together with recommendations for the improvement of ninth grade education.

The appendices include a discussion of the shadow study technique, together with lists of the schools, observers, and analysts.

CHAPTER 2

The Ninth Grader:
A Profile

What are ninth graders like? The question has something in common with the one asked by the Mongol emperor Kublai Khan of Marco Polo in 1275 when he inquired, "What is Europe like?" Polo stayed on for 24 years and spent much of his time answering Khan's question.

I believe I would need at least half that long to describe adequately the 14 and 15-year-old American youngster. Since it is necessary for the purposes of this study, however, to limit the description, I will present a profile of the ninth grader—some general characteristics that will serve as a guide for your understanding.

Profiles are only outlines, and outlines can be wanting. A ninth grade assignment to read *A Tale of Two Cities* is not really met by the student who chooses instead to read the Cliffs Notes summary of Dickens' novel. True, some facts are learned, but the texture, meaning, and excitement of the novel are lost in the outline.

This ninth grade profile should be regarded in the same way—some factual material, but without the flavor and richness of the real thing. However, this chapter should provide readers with a basic review of the ninth grader that will serve as a foundation for assessing the educational program offered this particular group of students.

If profiles are outlines, then they are also generalizations. Youngsters in the 14 to 15-year-old range share a common set of characteristics, but it should not be forgotten that there is a broad range of variation and that *these variations are significant for both the youngsters and the schools they attend.* The factors that cause these variations are numerous and include intelligence levels, rate of physical maturation, motivation, socio-economic status, and family make-up.

Further, both the significance and the definition of "variation" are not necessarily agreed upon if one includes (as one should) the opinions of the ninth graders themselves. A developmental psychologist might conclude that two 14-year-old girls are comparable in the rate of physical maturation based on data indicating similar height, weight, and onset of puberty; variation, therefore, being practically nonexistent. But the two young ladies— tape measure in hand—might violently disagree when a two-inch bust size difference emerges.

With these cautionary statements, let me now briefly summarize the physical, emotional, social, and cognitive status of the ninth grader.

This chapter was written by Joel Milgram, University of Cincinnati.

Physical Level of Development

The amount of physical change in adolescents is so great that it affects practically all other aspects of their home and school lives. It is also an area where the changes are nearly universal, yet, where differences between the sexes and variations among the same sex exist.

For most ninth graders the process of puberty began some time ago. The hypothalamus initiates the release of hormones which cause the development of the primary and secondary sex characteristics in both sexes. The girls began this process typically in the fifth and sixth grades, and the boys in the seventh and eighth grades.

Various hormones stimulate growth in both sexes, but sex differences result from different concentrations of the gonadal hormones. Males have greater amounts of the androgens which cause changes in the reproductive system. The estrogens and progesterone from the ovaries in the female contribute to the development of the reproductive system and secondary sex characteristics.

These hormonal changes produce dramatic external physical changes. The ninth grade female has already come close to her full adult height, and for some this has been true for the past two years. The ninth grade boy has more recently started his growth spurt and is pleased to find himself getting taller (at last) than his female counterpart.

The distribution of body weight is also different for 14 and 15-year-old youngsters. During the male growth spurt, shoulders became broader, and legs, compared with trunk length, grow longer. Girls lose less fat in their growth spurt and fat deposits occur in the breasts, thighs, and backs of upper arms.

With narrow shoulders, broader hips, and shorter legs relative to trunk size, their bodies have taken on a more rounded appearance.

While it is true that males eventually develop larger muscles than females, the age of 14 may not necessarily be the time to prove it. Girls attain their peak muscle growth *during* their height spurt, but boys achieve their peak in muscle development approximately one year *after* their growth spurt. Among ninth graders there may be a considerable number of girls who are stronger than their male peers.

The majority of girls at this age have already experienced their first period (menarche), pubic hair is fully developed, and breast development is nearly mature. Among the boys, most have developed enlarged testes and scrotum, though the genitalia may not yet be of adult size. In the ninth grade we may assume that approximately half the males have had nocturnal emissions. It is around this time that boys' sweat glands increase in size, contributing to facial acne and increased body odor.

Emotional Level of Development

The emotional status of the ninth grader is difficult to describe. But again, it is possible to make some generalizations.

Fourteen and 15-year-olds feel, and rightly so, that they have taken a giant step out of childhood. What they have stepped into is somewhat debatable. Their teachers and parents won't call it adulthood, and frankly, neither would the ninth grader.

But the ninth grader sees adulthood being much closer—and with good reason. Many have adult bodies, and getting a driver's license is just around the corner. Many of the girls are taller than their mothers, and the boys are looking down upon their father's balding heads. It is time for the search for a personal identity, and the process of achieving their identity will evoke a wide range of emotions, including self-doubt, conflict, experimentation, and confusion.

Tied to the search for personal identity is the desire to be more autonomous, to gain more control and power in governing the activities of life. What is termed *behavioral* autonomy is clearly demonstrated by many 14-year-olds. Keeping a part-time job and being involved in after-school activities are demonstrations of such autonomy.

Fewer have achieved *emotional* autonomy, and most are still highly dependent on parents for love and nurturance. The distinction between behavioral and emotional autonomy is often lost by parents, who may interpret a 14-year-old's drive for independence as a rejection of family love and concern.

The nature of the conflicts experienced by the ninth grader in the search for increased independence is strongly related to parenting practices. There are authoritarian homes where no choices exist for the youngster. For these adolescents, school may be the only place where choices exist. These choices are good for most, but it is also possible that some ninth graders simply cannot handle choices due to the lack of opportunity to practice making them in the home. Careful guidance for such youngsters is crucial.

The quest for identity and autonomy comes easily to some and not so easily to others. But for all, there will be moments of moodiness, misery, and depression. Too often, if parents are not understanding or if sensitive teachers are not available, the ninth grader can feel lonely, isolated, and ready to give up. Sometimes giving up means neglecting studies or dropping off a team or club. It can also mean striking back in a rebellious or destructive manner. Most often, however, ninth graders have good track records for pulling themselves out of depressions and optimistically continue with the struggle for self and independence.

Social Level of Development

Where ninth graders are socially has a lot to do with their physical and emotional development. The early maturing male will find himself given greater opportunities for athletics, interaction with girls, and leadership positions as compared with the late maturing male. The late maturer, perhaps deprived of such opportunities, may develop a negative self-concept with feelings of inadequacy, dependency, rejection, and rebelliousness. The dreaded compulsory shower in the locker room creates an unbelievable nightmare for the late maturer.

The early maturing girl does not have the same clearcut advantage as her male counterpart. Being regarded as older than her actual age, the early maturer often finds herself with older males and facing greater social pressure, especially in sexual matters. Other girls take their physical maturity to be an asset, just as early maturing boys do. Generally, however, whether an adolescent girl matures early or not does not influence her prestige among her peers, as it does for the early maturing boy.

As the importance of peers increases, the public denial of the importance of parents also increases. Sometimes it seems as if most ninth graders have no parents at all. Parents are often confused and hurt when their ninth grader simply refuses to be seen with them on the street.

It is not uncommon for a ninth grade youngster, being driven to school in a rain storm, to ask the parent to stop a block before school so the student may walk the rest of the way alone. Better wet than be seen with a parent.

Such behaviors are not as related to independence (notice that the ninth grader did not altogether *refuse* a ride on a rainy day) as they are to social appearances. One of the very important goals of many ninth graders is to prove to their peers that they are quickly becoming adults. Any public association with parents may be interpreted as a regression toward childhood. This is one of the reasons that ninth graders stay away from home as much as possible, and that some stay closeted in their rooms when they are home.

Although parents and family served as the primary model and reference group through middle childhood, the ninth grader strongly identifies with a peer group of friends who are similarly seeking their own identity. Most ninth graders are ready to join one of the many subcultures that exist in schools. Some groups emphasize studies and aspirations for college; others primarily stress dating, smoking, and the rejection of studies and school. Still another subculture is associated with athletics, popularity, and school activities. These subcultures (called by one researcher, the academic subculture, the delinquent subculture, and the fun subculture) are not necessarily related to any particular socio-economic class, and many adolescents participate to some degree in all three.

The function of the peer group is more than just to provide some independence from the family; it also serves as a reference group for judging one's own behavior and assists in clarifying one's personal identity.

Ninth grade friendships are an important part of the youngster's life. Generally at this age, the adolescent seeks out a same-sex friend in whom he or she can confide and trust. Girls tend to emphasize the satisfaction of emotional needs such as intimacy and dependency, while boys seek action-oriented relationships.

Many ninth graders begin dating, especially in the context of small-group activities. The increasing sexual interest and arousal is an integral part of their developing identity. Most adolescents at this age are likely to have liberal attitudes toward sex, but it should be remembered that their attitudes appear to be more liberal than their behavior.

Cognitive Level of Development

Piaget's theory of cognitive development still remains one of the dominant forces in American educational psychology. His four stages of development are seen as a continuous process with gradual transitions from one to the next. His final stage, called the period of formal operations, is reached by some at ages 11 or 12. It appears, therefore, that we can assume our ninth graders are prepared to deal with abstract reasoning and systematic experimentation—something they could not do when they were in the previous stage known as concrete operations.

If you are bothered by the fact that many ninth graders in your building do not appear to deal effectively with logic and abstract thinking, take comfort in the fact that a number of studies have shown a fairly high percentage of 14-year-olds are still testing in the concrete operational stage, meaning that they have difficulty in abstracting a general principle from a particular example.

Ninth graders are, of course, very much aware of their intellectual abilities relative to the school population. They have all seen their fair share of Metropolitan and Iowa tests and have looked at bars and stars and shaded areas showing them where they stand in their school, in their state, and in their country.

Most standardized tests sample a restricted range of cognitive abilities that primarily apply to school learning, but cognitive development also applies to the thinking skills necessary for social interaction. Two concepts related to social cognition are particularly worth noting since they apply so strongly to many ninth graders.

The first is called the "imaginary audience," and occurs when the adolescent believes that he or she is constantly being observed because of his general importance. This being the case we can appreciate the teenagers who wash their hair twice before coming to school and spend every free moment in school combing and grooming themselves. After all, how much longer would you spend in front of a mirror if you believed that everyone in the school building was constantly watching you? While the "imaginary audience" concept may result in heightened self-consciousness and concern for one's appearance, it can also result in excessive shyness and increased need for privacy.

8

Finally, one must be aware of the concept of the "personal fable," which involves the overexaggeration of the adolescents' own uniqueness both in feelings and immortality. They come to regard themselves as very special and unique and, while teachers and parents often encourage these feelings, the ninth graders typically take them to excess. It can lead to dangerous risk-taking, but more often simply to boorish behavior dripping with egocentric mannerisms.

From the profile described above, it becomes fairly obvious that ninth graders have certain needs which schools can and should help meet.

As we observe the variations in physical development, it becomes clear that well-rounded recreational programs should be part of physical education. Athletic activities should be available to all, but mostly for the purpose of fun rather than for competitive awards. Non-athletic boys and girls must not be excluded from enjoying physical activities which are important for both physical and mental health.

Emotionally, ninth graders need sensitive and understanding teachers. Their depressions and moods should be viewed in the context of their drastically changing lives. Encouraging, supportive teachers help considerably in the hard struggle for emotional maturity.

Socially, ninth graders will seek out friendships, and schools must accept the fact that the school building *is* a place for socialization. Teachers and administrators also become the socialization agents, for it is they who bring the students together in classes, clubs, and lunchrooms. Making sure that the school building is a place for learning, as well, is both the challenge and the need.

As far as cognitive development is concerned we should remember that ninth graders do want to learn—they are in fact eager learners—but their need is to be challenged. This is not always an easy task. To what extent ninth graders are challenged will be revealed in later chapters.

CHAPTER 3

What Are Ninth Graders Experiencing in School?

In education, as in athletics, onlookers often have a better view of the activities than do the participants. To get, then, a good view of what ninth graders actually were experiencing in school, 141 "onlookers" carefully watched and recorded the experiences of 141 randomly-selected ninth graders on one day in March, 1984.

These candid pictures of the educational experiences, presented from the consumer's viewpoint, are most revealing. This chapter presents the summarized picture of what a school day in the life of a ninth grader is like.

No matter in what state or region they are located, ninth graders have quite similar experiences. The rituals of school are well established in our culture. Although there are some exceptions and many variations, ninth graders all experience buses, lockers, textbooks, notebooks, changing classes, seatwork, board work, roll call, gym, homework, lunch period, listening, subject-centered classes, and sitting—quite a lot of sitting.

On March 7, 1984, all of these characteristics of schooling in America were very evident. There did exist, however, a number of breaks in the usual routine. In one school, "Club Day" necessitated the shortening of each of the regular periods by a few minutes; in another "Hat Day," a part of Spirit Week, was being held. In still another the celebration of Foreign Language Week resulted in many items throughout the school being labeled in a foreign language and students exchanging greetings in other languages.

In one school, the entire morning was taken up with state standardized tests. Field trips were being conducted in a few schools, and one physical education class was bused to the downtown bowling alley. The longest bus ride, however, was surely that one experienced by the son of a rancher in the west who traveled 180 miles a day to attend school!

In many respects, these variations only served to highlight the overall sameness of our educational enterprise. There were clear differences in quality, to be sure, but the program structure, the content, and the trappings were pretty much the same. A visitor from another land, after visiting schools across the country, might well assume that we had a national school system rather than 50 state systems.

The 141 schools in which shadow studies were conducted included 45 junior high schools, 71 high schools, and 25 junior-senior high schools. Schools from 48 states and the District of Columbia were included in the sample.

Four out of five of the junior high schools enrolled fewer than 1,000 students, while approximately two out of three of the high schools enrolled more than 1,000 students. The junior-senior high schools, as would be expected, were the smallest of all; more than a third of them enrolled fewer than 500 students. One school had only an average of 20 pupils per grade level.

The junior high schools were likely to be located in cities and suburban areas, while the high schools were usually in small towns, suburban areas, and large cities. Junior-senior high schools were located predominantly in small towns and rural areas.

The school day in the junior-senior high schools and in the junior high schools typically consisted of seven periods, while a six-period day was the median in 9-12 schools. An eight-period day was occasionally found in all school types.

Utilizing the analysts' reports as prime data sources, but supplemented by references to the original 141 reports themselves, the reality of the ninth grade is described in the following sections. The 10 aspects of a school program that were used by the analysts in organizing their reports are employed as a framework for describing the nature of the experiences ninth graders underwent on March 7, 1984.

A. *Instructional Program-Content*

The content of the ninth grade is very traditional and quite standard. Both observers and analysts often commented on the similarity of what was being studied to what they had studied 20 or 30 years ago. The basic subjects of English, mathematics, social studies, and science were nearly always present.

("The 20 observers generally described traditional curriculum areas." "The context, except for the inclusion of some computer education, is traditional. It appears to be a 1931 program in a 1931 building." "The curriculum content in these sample classes reflects a traditional 'subject matter' emphasis wherein students learn content and demonstrate knowledge on tests.")

Beyond the "big four" courses, physical education ranked next in frequency. It was usually offered, but not necessarily for a full year. The most common course electives were home economics, industrial arts, art, and music. Foreign language was usually offered and was sometimes required.

Although a few observers expressed the opinion that the content was appropriate ("Curriculum content appeared to be meeting the needs of the students selected"), far more typical were comments concerning the limited attention to exploration or to diverse student needs.

("Few attempts were made to provide exploratory or student-centered activities." "Students have limited time for exploratory courses of personal interest to them." "More variety needs to be offered to deal with our ever changing world." "There is little, if any, opportunity for exploratory curriculum activities in grade nine.")

B. *Teaching Arrangements*

Departmentalized. No other word is needed to cover this aspect of the ninth grade program. Only three observers noted anything other than straight departmentalization as the way the program was organized for instruction. It was probably the most universal characteristic noted by the 141 observers.

This generalization was confirmed by the information provided on the general information form that each school completed. Irrespective of the grade pattern, departmentalization was clearly the instructional organization order of the day.

But beyond recognizing the mere existence of departmentalization, many observers and analysts noted the lack of any correlation between subjects or any evidence of an awareness by teachers of what content other teachers were presenting. One student had three major subject tests on March 7.

The word *fragmented* was often cited as characteristic. ("No evidence of cooperative planning among teachers." "No team teaching, block scheduling, or interdisciplinary   11 instruction." "Learning appeared to occur in segments.") One observer described the school day as "a series of short vignettes—nothing seemed to be deep or ongoing, but rather skipping from one to another."

Ability grouping or tracking seemed to be common in most of the sites studied.

C. *Instruction and Teaching Methods*

The lecture method continues to dominate the instructional procedures employed in the ninth grade. ("Nearly all classes consist of teachers talking to classes." "The lecture method was the primary instructional mode." "Almost all observers described the traditional lecture-chalkboard developmental lesson type instruction method of teaching." "Ninety-five percent of instruction is didactic lecture-note taking. Teacher dominates the process with little student participation other than the typical student feedback.")

Such lecturing, however, was sometimes noted as being of high quality. ("The teaching is traditional and of fairly high quality. Generally teachers get very high marks.")

Also frequently noted as an instructional technique was seatwork. This often involved answering questions or working on homework assignments for the next day. Having several students go to the board to do a problem, correct or translate a sentence, or engage in some comparable activity was common. Going over homework was sometimes cited as taking an inordinate amount of time.

Laboratory approaches and small-group work were noted primarily because they were infrequent.

D. *Teacher-Student Interaction*

Teacher-student interaction was limited primarily to the content at hand. This generalization was widely stated in one form or another by nearly every analyst. ("Interaction between teachers and students seemed positive but limited primarily to the subject matter being taught." "There appears to be almost no informal student-teacher interaction." "Virtually none." "Respectful, but very limited.")

Concern over the lack of real interaction, even about the subject matter at hand, was regularly expressed by both individual observers and analysts. Students were not asked to express their ideas.

What interaction did occur was almost always initiated by the teacher asking a question that was directed to the class or to an individual. Numerous observers reported that their student did not interact with the teacher at all. As one observer phrased it, "Unless actively pursues attention he/she may not get it."

This was especially characteristic of "good" students; those that are neither disruptive and off-task nor outstanding and aggressive. One observer expressed this concern effectively in these statements: "This student is considered a jewel by her teachers. Nonetheless, there was little evidence of intellectual challenge. She simply remained comfortable in her day. I felt, at times, that she could have permitted herself to be challenged, but that would involve some discomfort. Our program—perhaps our schools in general—do not encourage growth by challenge and confrontation."

At the same time, observers and analysts pointed out that students saw their teachers as caring, helpful people. Teachers were patient. Students were respectful.

E. *Student-Student Interaction*

Ninth grade students like to talk. The out-of-class interaction of students with one another was enthusiastic, friendly, and nearly constant. Any available moment is seized for peer contact and conversation. The topics during such informal contacts focus more on people than on academic matters, although, like the weather among adults, comments on the status of homework are easy openers for a conversation.

12

Lunch seems to be the highlight of the day, for here nearly uninhibited socialization is possible, and the opportunity is eagerly exploited. Students who in class seem passive and lethargic come alive during lunch period. This break in the schedule may be as important for its social nature as for its physical sustenance. Informal groupings still tend to be composed of the same sex, although some mixed groups were noted.

The few minutes available between the actual eating of lunch and the end of the period provide a needed opportunity for considerable physical activity and movement. An observer, while noting the noisy lunch period, concluded, "After it was over there was very little evidence of the energy that was released during the 35 minutes."

Comments noting that students were well behaved, though occasionally boisterous during their out-of class opportunities for socialization, were frequent. Students seem to respect their peers and adults as well.

The in-class interaction of students was, of course, more restrained. Students did talk to one another frequently during class; however, such contacts were done covertly, seemingly in violation of class standards. They tended to whisper and try not to bring attention to themselves. Ninth graders have not completely given up the practice of note passing. At the same time, they are also becoming adept at nonverbal communication.

There were limited instances of student-student interaction on a planned basis within the classroom. ("It was clear that student-student interaction was definitely not meant to be a part of the student's day. . . .") There were, however, instances of student-student interaction in science labs and in some small-group work.

F. *Physical Environment*

The physical environment of most schools was described as adequate. However, wide variances existed in the quality of physical arrangements. Buildings were described as comfortable, clean, and cheerful; or as old and worn, dirty and cold. The overall physical condition and maintenance of the building was not a matter on which observers were expected to comment, although a good many did, usually in positive tones.

Descriptions of the physical condition of individual classrooms were varied. ("Rooms were bright, cheerful, and well-decorated with meaningful bulletin boards." "In almost all cases, students sat in desks arranged in rows or at standard lab tables." "Sterile and drab.")

Comments on the efforts of teachers to make rooms conducive to learning were frequent, while negative comments about the classrooms were limited.

For the most part, observers did not feel that the nature of the physical environment interfered with the learning process. ("The physical environment does not appear to have an influence one way or the other on one's ability to learn." "Not criticized by students. Generally did not appear to be a problem." "Teacher attention to environment is noticed and appreciated by students.")

On the other hand, there was little indication that the physical environment facilitated learning. ("There is wide variation in detail, but not essence.")

Furniture adaptations to facilitate informal learning were rarely noted. ("Limited situation of tables and chairs for small-group interaction." "Seating arrangements show little variation regardless of task." "Five rows of six or six rows of five seem to be the norm with very little creative grouping.")

G. *Advising and Counseling*

A single day's activities may not be a sufficient basis for judging a school's advising and counseling program, and very few observers noted any evidence of a counseling program. ("There was no apparent advisement or counseling during the day in any of the studies I read." "Little evidence of this activity." "Advising and counseling were mentioned by only one observer.")

On the other hand, in student interviews at the end of the day, many students identified a counselor as one to whom they would go for advice with a specific problem. They seemed fully aware of the availability of counselors.

There were no reports of group or developmental counseling, of adviser-advisee programs (with one clear and two possible exceptions), or other indications that comprehensive guidance services were a part of ninth grade programs. Particularly noticeable was the fact that apparently all counseling was undertaken at the student's initiative rather than at the initiative of the school.

Counseling, it appears, is still viewed as essentially remedial rather than developmental, and it is directed toward the solution of problems more than toward prevention through the acquisition of coping skills and the achievement of more adequate personal adjustment.

The speculations of both observers and analysts regarding the limited extent of counseling activities apparent proved to be correct when related data were drawn from the information sheet. The schools reported their enrollments and were asked to describe their counseling services for ninth graders.

All schools reported the availability of counseling services. However, it is clear that few schools, regardless of type, are in a position to do a great deal of preventive and developmental counseling.

The student to counselor ratios existing are staggering. In one case, only one counselor was available to serve 1,500 students. In another, the ratio was one for 1,200 students. More typical were ratios in the 350 to 500 students for each counselor. One school reported a to-be-envied ratio of one to 75.

Career planning and orientation programs were often cited on the information sheet as responsibilities of counselors.

H. *Opportunities for Social Skill Learning*

Observers and analysts report an almost complete lack of planned activities directed toward the learning of social skills. ("Little evidence existed of any opportunities for social skill learning other than in the cafeteria." "No planned opportunities for social skill learning were noted by observers." "Very little, if any, opportunity for social skill learning appears to be built into the program." "Limited indication of social skill development, mainly through activity types of classes including gym and music programs.")

There are abundant informal opportunities for practicing social skills. In such situations, however, learning is by trial and error and via peers.

Even though there is apparently little assistance given ninth graders in the cultivation of desirable social skills, their social competence was reported as high by many observers. Students were at ease with one another and with themselves. They appeared to have little difficulty relating to each other or to their teachers.

I. *Teacher and Student Use of Class Time*

Wide variations existed in observations about how class time was used. A few observers noted that every moment was filled; others reported large gaps when students were left without direction or purpose.

All analysts agreed that the majority of class time was devoted to teacher talk and to the presentation of information. ("Teachers are mainly involved in presentation of lecture data and students in listening and note taking." "Teachers mainly spent their time lecturing, answering questions, or giving assignments. Students spent most of their time listening, taking tests, or answering teacher-generated questions.")

Some observers noted that much classroom time remained unfilled. ("Teachers did not always plan to fill the instructional time and let students do homework in class, read, or have free time.")

14

For the most part, however, class time was devoted to instruction. Students seemed prepared, ready to engage in the activity of the day, and task oriented. In fact, students were often described as passive and pliable, willing to undertake virtually any assignment given. The use of class time seemed to vary with the ability of the teacher and the time of day.

Several observers felt the less able students were being overlooked. One analyst pointed out that "while teachers would feel that class time is used effectively, student use of time would belie this. It is possible for a student to 'sleep through' many classes because he/she is never called or made to be accountable."

J. *School Learning Climate*

The school learning climate was often described as purposeful. Students were engaged in learning tasks as directed by their teachers. ("Most reports implied a conscientious approach to learning among teachers and students." "Students and teachers both seemed to have a positive attitude toward learning." "The school learning climate appeared to be positive." "Good school learning climate existing in most cases." "The school climate is teacher dominated, but friendly, comfortable, and supportive.")

Although academics appeared to be valued, many observers cited their students as being bored and uninterested. Lack of challenge was often noted. ("Educators are keeping most students well occupied, but they are not being stimulated and challenged properly.")

One of the clearest generalizations emerging from the shadow studies was the overall excellence of student behavior. The schools ninth graders attend are civil places. Both observers and analysts regularly commented, often with surprise, that discipline was not the problem many assume it to be. One observer said: "During the entire day I did not see a single incident of disruptive or disrespectful behavior. I had been led to believe that ninth graders can be outrageous in both respects and usually are. Obviously this is not always true."

One observer, however, did make a strongly negative comment regarding student behavior (". . . students who were cooperative had to contend with the constant chatter of fellow students, students calling out, talking back to and shouting at the teachers. . . . I am horrified and appalled at what has been accepted as the norm by the teachers. . . .")

Some observers and analysts expressed the view that the generally good behavior students exhibited was not because of, but in spite of, the rather dull teaching procedures employed.

Several observers commented that the attention span of ninth graders was clearly longer than that of seventh and eighth graders, as was their ability to work without constant direction and reassurance.

What Students Think About Their Schools

The end-of-day interviews provided considerable data regarding the perceptions of students toward their teachers and their school. While students had no real basis for making comparative judgments, and a limited perspective by which to assess the effectiveness of their educational experiences, their opinions are important. Their perceptions are, for them, the truth on which they base their behavior.

Both teachers and schools score very high marks from ninth grade students. When asked what they like best about their schools, kids (or friends) and teachers were definitely the two responses most frequently cited, with kids winning out by only a small margin. ("The friends I've made." "My teachers always encourage me." "Friends to talk to and to be with; they make the day go faster.")

Other responses included "people," "my counselor," "activities," "computers," "physical education," "sports," and "the choices I have." The particular school activity or athletic program that the student was involved in was regularly mentioned as the "best thing" about school.

When asked, "what one thing would you change about the school if you could?" they had much more difficulty coming up with an answer.

Many said "nothing" or that they couldn't think of anything. The lunches, of course, came in for some criticism, but not as much as might be expected. Several spoke of the need for more school spirit or more choices of courses.

"Put doors on the restrooms," "more free time," and "it could be cleaner," were among the responses. One boy went so far as to say "get a new school and cancel out I.P.S. science." Only one junior high student expressed the opinion that the ninth grade should be in the high school.

On the question about "the best thing that happened to you today," responses, for the most part, fell into two categories—social or personal, and academic. ("Having lunch with my friends." "I got interviewed." "The counselor complimented me." "I asked a girl out on a date today and she said yes." "I made a B+ on a science test." "I got a C in math; I usually do worse." "Science was fun.")

On the related question about the best thing that happened this year, the same two categories prevailed. ("I made cheerleading." "My boy friend." "Being in the fall production." "Most tackles in football." "Band." "Honor roll." "Received the first A I ever made." "Improving my grade in Algebra.")

Citing the worst thing that happened today and this year seemed to cause a bit more difficulty, but answers were in much the same vein. ("Fell off the bottom step of bus into snow." "Too shy to give note to girl I like." "Don't understand science." "Those tests." "Getting into a fight." "Starting out the day with math.")

When asked how they would describe their school to a newcomer, students were usually positive, often lavish in their praise. ("This is the best school in the state." "The best junior high school in the city." "I wouldn't trade my school for anything.")

Slightly qualified compliments were very common. ("It's a pretty good school." "The teachers are pretty nice." "If you don't narc and get other people in trouble, it's a real fun place." "People are friendly." "It's not a prep school." "Prepares you for high school—a lot of extra activities.")

One junior high student offered this interesting analysis: "This school is like a soap opera—everybody knows everything. There are a lot of social things happening—everybody's into something."

When queried as to whether or not there was someone in the school they would turn to if they needed help with a personal problem, students mentioned friends, teachers, and counselors. They usually named a particular teacher or counselor. Those in athletics often mentioned a coach, as it is known that coaches become important models and advisers to their players. Some students indicated they would go to their parents if they had a serious problem.

All in all, there was little doubt about the positive perceptions students hold of their teachers and their schools. Evident in nearly all of their responses was a recognition of the importance of the human element. Schools simply have a built-in advantage—they are filled with people!

A good many observers noted that while their own assessment of the school program was lukewarm, the evaluation of the student was completely positive. However incomplete or inadequate a school may be from the standpoint of the professional educator, the students who attend like it.

Does Organizational Pattern Affect Program?

T he question presented as the chapter title elicits considerable interest. Many educators, affiliated with one type of organizational unit or another and with a long-held opinion on the issue, are as interested in this matter as they are in the general status of ninth grade programs.

For all such educators, the results of this study will be disappointing.

Does organizational pattern affect program? In a word, *no*. There are a few distinctions and differences between school types: The major finding of the comparative analysis is that the ninth grader's day in a junior high school is comparable to a ninth grader's day in a four-year senior high school or in a junior-senior high school.

There simply were no significant differences revealed in the program conditions evaluated. The differences that did exist were largely ones that involved out-of-class or extracurricular activities and were revealed in the school information sheets rather than in the reports of the school days.

Before further discussion of the findings, an explanation of the procedure used in conducting the comparative analysis is in order. As noted in the first chapter, 26 educators were invited to share in this activity. These educators were asked to review and suggest changes on a checklist of program conditions that would be used in evaluating individual shadow studies. The original list, developed by the NASSP Middle Level Council and Committee, contained items that might be desirable in a ninth grade program.

Based on the revisions and additions analysts suggested, a final checklist of 18 items was prepared. Each analyst then received a group of 10 or 11 shadow studies, randomly grouped, and was asked to complete a checklist for each study that would indicate the degree to which a certain program condition was evident in that study. The grade organization pattern of the shadow studies was not known by the analysts, although they were aware of the purpose of the ratings.

This procedure resulted in each shadow study being scored twice. When returned, these checklists were categorized according to school type and tabulated, which made it possible to compare school organizational types with one another.

The analysts or raters were asked to score each shadow study on the 18 dimensions using the following scale:

3 = ample evidence that the program condition is present;
2 = some evidence that the program condition is present;
1 = little or no evidence that the program condition is present.

The mean rating given each type of school on each of the 18 program conditions is shown in Table 1. Even a cursory glance at the figures reveals that there are few differences among school organizational types involving program conditions frequently cited as desirable for middle level schools.

Table I

Mean Rating on Presence of Program Conditions for Each Organizational Type

Program Conditions	Group X		
	N = 80 (7-9)	120 (9-12)	38 (7-12)
1. Did the student participate in instructional groups of various sizes (full class, small group, pairs, large group)?	1.88	1.85	2.00
2. Did the student participate in instructional groups of different types (homogeneous, heterogeneous, interest centered)?	1.53	1.63	1.65
3. Did the day include any opportunities for addressing the personal-social needs of students?	1.76	1.64	1.69
4. Did the student receive direct instruction in skill areas such as reading or writing?	1.76	1.65	1.75
5. Was the subject matter studied related to here and now?	1.52	1.47	1.73
6. Did the physical education activities recognize and accommodate the varied levels of development?	1.55	1.68	1.58
7. Did the physical education activities recognize the leisure time and likely future of activities?	1.61	1.73	1.63
8. Did the student participate in activities or deal with content that related to careers?	1.39	1.26	1.47
9. Did the student participate in exploratory activities which helped him or her ascertain aptitudes and interests?	1.60	1.53	1.68
10. Was the community utilized as a resource either by a resource person, field trip, or related activity?	2.01	2.02	2.26
11. Was the student recognized individually by at least one teacher during the day?	1.24	1.22	1.35
12. Did student-teacher planning occur during the day?	1.45	1.38	1.45
13. Was the student involved in situations calling for value discrimination, critical thinking, or analysis of options?	1.70	1.58	1.78
14. Did the day include an opportunity for personalized, individualized instruction or learning?	1.45	1.42	1.53

| | Group X | | |
Program Conditions	N = 80 (7-9)	120 (9-12)	38 (7-12)
15. Did the student have opportunity to elect or select anything in his or her learning activities?	1.67	1.63	1.84
16. Did the student initiate conversation with a teacher during class or outside of class?	1.32	1.45	1.37
17. Was the student complimented by a peer or teacher during the day?	1.95	1.92	2.18
18. Did the student have any time to be alone, to reflect as an individual, during the day?	2.10	2.06	3.11

1 = little or no evidence of the principle
2 = some evidence of the principle
3 = a great deal of evidence

As notable as the lack of differences among school organizational types is the evident lack of these practices in *all* of the schools, despite their organizational structure. On an absolute scale, only 3 of the 18 conditions approach a rating of 2, and thus show "some evidence" of being present in the schools: the use of the community as a resource (item 10); the complimenting of students by peers or teachers (item 17); and the provision of time for the student to be alone (item 18). All the rest of the items fail to rise much above the little or no evidence category.

Of course, it can be argued that these conditions might not be evident to an observer who spends only one day in the building. However, because the observers were trained, professional educators who are familiar with even the most subtle nuances of school operations, and because of the consistency with which references to these conditions fail to appear in their reports, it is possible to have some confidence in these findings.

And most important, the observations were conducted from a point of view which tried to emulate that of ninth grade students. That means that in spite of the best intentions of school people to provide these conditions, they are not evident from a student's point of view—the one that counts most.

Were there any differences at all? Some, but they may not be attributable to school organization. On six items (5, 8, 10, 11, 15, 17), slight differences can be observed between 7-12 schools and both 7-9 and 9-12 schools.

On item 5, "Was the subject matter related to the here and now?" 7-12 schools scored somewhat higher than either 7-9 or 9-12 schools. This seems to be related to two other questions in which the same pattern of responses is evident: question 8 ("Did the student participate in activities or deal with content that related to careers?"), and question 10 ("Was the community used as a resource either by a resource person, field trip, or related activity?"). This suggests that 7-12 schools are *slightly* more likely to provide relevant curricula, an orientation to careers, and a connection with the community.

Is this because they are 7-12 schools? Probably not. Schools that house grades 7-12 tend to be considerably smaller in size and are located in smaller communities than either 9-12 or 7-9 schools. Therefore, the outcomes on the items noted above may be more indigenous to smaller communities than to larger ones.

Schools in small towns or rural locations *do* tend to be more closely connected to the communities they serve than are schools in larger cities or sprawling suburbs. Therefore, a 19 fairly distinct career orientation—linked to the career options of the community and reinforced by both the curriculum and the presence of community resources—is easy to imagine in a 7-12 setting.

The other differences, all favoring the 7-12 school, seem to support the hypothesis that the differences arise from community size rather than organizational plan as well. Item 11 ("Was the student recognized individually by at least one teacher during the day?"), item 15 ("Did the student have the opportunity to elect or select anything in his or her learning activities?"), and item 17 ("Was the student complimented by a peer or teacher during the day?") all produced results which favored, again slightly, the 7-12 organization.

This outcome isn't surprising because of the nature of the items: All deal with some form of social interaction that is more easily managed in a small setting than a larger one. Items 11 and 17, in particular, deal with a style of social exchange that is more likely to be found in institutions where the inhabitants know and interact with each other outside of the institutional setting, such as in churches, clubs, or the supermarket, on a regular basis. These conditions, of course, are more characteristic of smaller towns than of large cities or suburbs.

Item 15, dealing with student choice, may also be a function of school and community size. Smaller schools, the research tells us, tend to be better able to respond to individual needs and make special arrangements for students than do larger ones. Principals and teachers have more autonomy in smaller school organizations and are less bound than their big-city colleagues by complex districtwide policies and regulations.

Confirming Analysis

In order to confirm the conclusions that appeared evident by direct inspection of the data, a secondary analysis was performed.

A factor analysis was conducted on the 18 questionnaire items. This analysis yielded four factors which accounted for nearly 60 percent of the sample variance. These factors focused on curriculum and instruction, interpersonal relationships, physical education, and social climate.

A multivariate analysis of variance was then conducted in which the school type was treated as the independent variable and each school's score on the factors listed above the dependent variable. The analysis showed that there were no significant differences among any of the school organizational types on any of the factors studied. Clearly, the school organization type in which the ninth grade is housed has no systematic effect on the program elements examined in this study.

Perhaps the most important part of this analysis is not what it tells us about comparative aspects of school organization plans, but what it tells us about the presence of certain desirable conditions in absolute terms. As mentioned earlier, only three items were noted as having "some evidence" of being part of the school program. Conversely, that suggests that the remaining 15 items were not very prevalent at all.

Eight items in particular were cited as showing "little or no" evidence of being part of a ninth grader's program: 2, 5, 6, 8, 11, 12, 14, and 16. Four of these items (2, 6, 12, 14) are related to instruction, two focus on curriculum (5, 8), and two focus on interpersonal relationships (11, 16).

The items related to instruction showed that ninth grade students were not likely to participate in instructional groups of different types; in fact, they were not likely to receive much personalized, individualized instruction at all. There was little evidence that physical education activities recognized and accommodated varied levels of development, or that joint student-teacher planning occurred during the school day. In the area of curriculum,

20

the subject matter was not specifically related to the "here and now," and not much instruction seemed to be related to careers.

The lowest ranked item of all (11) shows that students are not likely to be recognized individually by at least one teacher during the school day. But neither are they likely to initiate a conversation with a teacher during class or outside of class. Despite the cordiality of student-teacher relationships reported elsewhere in this report, the amount of interaction between teachers and students seems to be limited and its purposes carefully circumscribed. Little of this interaction is initiated by students.

Differences Revealed from Data Sheets

The most revealing items on the basic data sheet that was completed by each of the 141 schools were those dealing with student activities. School personnel were asked to estimate the percentage of ninth graders who participated in student activities such as clubs, musical groups, and student government; the percentage who participated in intramurals; and the percentage who participated in interscholastic athletics. While figures given are often "guesstimates" and likely to be somewhat inaccurate, a few clear and important realities emerged when these data were tabulated.

Table II summarizes these data. The figures reveal that while the percent of ninth graders participating in interscholastic sports is relatively the same no matter what the school organization type, the percent of ninth graders who participate in student activities varies markedly according to grade level organization.

Table II

Percent of Ninth Graders Participating in
Student Activities, Intramurals, and Interscholastics by School Type

	% of Students Participating	School Type		
		9-12	7-9	7-12
Student Activities,	- 0	0	0	0
Clubs, etc.	1- 24	19	7	17
	25- 49	55	33	13
	50- 74	17	36	44
	75-100	9	24	26
	- 0	2	11	0
	1- 24	27	22	13
Interscholastics	25- 49	48	44	37
	50- 74	21	20	37
	75-100	2	2	13
	- 0	61	31	60
	1- 24	31	29	13
Intramurals	25- 49	6	22	9
	50- 74	0	11	9
	75-100	2	7	9

21

Ninth graders are much more likely to participate in activities in junior high schools and junior-senior high schools than in four year high schools, according to these figures. This conclusion is not surprising, for logic would lead one to assume that "freshmen" would be relatively inactive in clubs and activities that are inevitably dominated by upper classmen.

Equally logical would be the lower participation in intramurals by ninth graders in senior high schools, where such programs are seldom provided. Somewhat disappointing, it might be noted, is the level of participation reported in intramurals in all school types. Despite a rather universal advocacy of such programs they are still not extensive.

Clearly, the organizational variables that have for so long fascinated educators have little effect on the lives (or programs) of ninth grade students. They probably belong in the high school because of the opportunities afforded them there. But convincing arguments can be mustered for a junior high school placement as well. The final conclusion is that no organizational pattern is inherently better than any other in meeting the needs of ninth graders.

CHAPTER 5

Six Samples
of Reality

On March 7, 1984 some five million ninth graders attended school in the United States. Many went to separate junior high schools, others to combination junior-senior high schools, and still others to four-year high schools. A few attended a twelfth grade school or other organizational arrangement.

They rode buses, walked, or were driven. They usually carried an armful of books and notebooks, though one should not conclude that they had studied them the previous evening. These 14 and 15-year-old youngsters gathered in small groups, conversed with considerable animation, and generally seemed to be enjoying life.

The weather on March 7 was sunny throughout most of the nation, but snow fell in the Eastern plains and parts of the Midwest. Anchorage, Alaska recorded a high of 43°, while Orlando, Fla., was a warm 77°. It never got above 36° under the arch in St. Louis, Mo., and the temperature hovered around 20° all day in Des Moines, Iowa.

Democratic presidential candidates Walter Mondale and Gary Hart were campaigning for the South's upcoming primaries. On Capitol Hill in Washington, a compromise school prayer amendment was being negotiated.

For nearly all the ninth graders it was just another day of school. For 141 of them, however, that day was special. Although they were unaware of it, their school day would be observed and recorded to provide data to answer the question, How fares the ninth grade?

This chapter is composed of six of those shadow studies. Identifying data have been omitted, but otherwise the studies are as they were submitted. The particular studies included were selected as "representative." They are neither the most positive nor the most negative. They are, obviously, ones which were reasonably complete and which evidenced a degree of perceptiveness. Intentionally, three of the studies included are 9-12 high schools, two are separate junior high schools, and one is a 7-12 combination junior-senior high school, a ratio which is roughly comparable to the total sample and the total population.

Shadow Study Number 1

Conducted in a city high school of more than 1,500 pupils in grades 9-12. The student was 15 years old and was classified as above average.

Time	Specific behavior at 5-7 minute intervals	Environment	Impression-Comments
8:51	S. came to class early, was typing on an assignment before class began.	Classroom is a typical typing classroom. There are a few more typewriters than is comfortable for the room size.	Students range from grade 9-12. Entered room quietly and began work right away.
8:58	S. having some difficulty on warm-up exercises. Making mistakes.	The number of typewriters makes the room very noisy.	No one seemed to be bothered by my presence. A few curious looks but no further attention.
9:01	S. is slower typing specific examples than rest of class.	Everyone is busy and seems on task.	Students are typing exercises from textbook. Many are very good and type quite rapidly.
9:08	S. is on task. Is typing a manuscript and stops to correct errors frequently.	Students on task and busy.	Teacher goes around classroom frequently and evaluates and helps students.
9:10	S. takes paper up to teacher for a critique. Is told to go on to page two but, if time, to correct some slight problems on page one. Seems fairly noncommital about it all.	Class continues typing.	Students are on task and busy.
9:16	S. stops work to listen to the teacher talking to the students near him. Asks teacher a question and goes back to work.	Students busy typing.	This class is very boring for an observer.
9:23	S. still working, but still making frequent corrections—at least one correction per minute. This is not a timed exercise, but an assignment for accuracy of typing skills.	Everyone continues on task.	Students seem to take their efforts very seriously.
9:30	S. still correcting errors. Does not, however, show any impatience or frustration.	Students still working on lesson.	Some students beginning to look around as period nears end.
9:37	S. still plugging away at page two.	Teacher helping individual students.	Some students ready for class to end.
9:41	S. makes final correction and puts work away. Talks quietly to neighbor.	Teacher tells students to finish up and get ready to leave.	Students are ready to go, and talk quietly until bell.

Time	Specific behavior at 5-7 minute intervals	Environment	Impressions-Comments
9:45	S. much more relaxed and active before class begins. Stands talking to friends. Complains about the job done in typing.	Clean and neat classroom. Very small class size. Sixteen students. Students listen to announcements.	Students are ready, go to work when bell rings.
9:52	S. plays with fingers as teacher explains lesson for the day. Begins reading quiz and asks a clarification question.	Teacher is explaining quiz and filmstrip on India.	Students are looking for ways to get teacher off task by asking irrelevant questions.
10:00	S. is watching filmstrip and taking notes.	Teacher is running filmstrip projector.	Students are attentive and taking notes. This is very difficult because room is dark.
10:07	S. continues to take notes on filmstrip.	The room is too dark to take good notes.	The environment is not conducive to accomplish the goals the teacher has set.
10:11	S. answers question correctly. Volunteers frequently to answer questions about filmstrip.	Class is attentive and on task.	The students seem to realize that stalling teacher is useless and it is time to get busy on test.
10:16	S. finishes quiz and throws notes away. Returns to seat and sits quietly.	Other students begin to finish quiz.	Room is very cold and impersonal. Few bulletin boards or displays. Any subject could be taught in this room.
10:23	S. reviews his notebook as teacher tells what to study for the final on March 20.	Students follow along and ask questions about the final.	It seems a little soon to begin reviewing for a final on March 20.
10:30	S. continues to follow along in his notebook as teacher reviews what should be studied for the final.	Students are listening and following along surprisingly well.	Teacher talks in a monotone and could easily put me to sleep. No wonder students dislike social studies.
10:37	S. begins to take notes as teacher begins to read sentences to be copied.	Students listen and write in notebooks as teacher reads from notes.	All information given by teacher for 15 minutes could have been on a mimeographed sheet and handed out in a couple of minutes. The dictation could also have been handed out for insertion in the notebook.
10:40	S. leans back and relaxes as he talks quietly and waits for 10:42 bell.	Students prepare to leave class and talk quietly.	Unimpressive class.

Time	Specific behavior at 5-7 minute intervals	Environment	Impressions-Comments
10:48	S. is in seat and listening to teacher describe material to be covered during the class.	Classroom is personal and friendly.	Students are well behaved and ready to go to work. My presence seems unnoticed.
10:52	S. begins answering quiz questions on a Scan-tron sheet.	Teacher is seated at front of class correcting papers.	Students seem prepared for quiz.
10:54	S. hands in answer sheet to quiz and returns to seat. Sits quietly.	Teacher talks quietly to other students about last night's activities.	Students quietly wait for everyone to finish quiz.
11:00	S. begins to take notes as teacher dictates material.	Students listen and write as teacher dictates.	This is supposed to improve listening skills. Seems to test speed of writing.
11:01	S. sharpens pencil and falls behind.		
11:08	S. continues to copy dictation as the teacher reads it.	Class is attentive and busy copying dictation.	If the objective is listening, it is being accomplished.
11:15	S. copies general questions for the final test as the teacher dictates.	Students are attentive and listening as teacher explains the meaning of each question for the library unit.	The objective is again to develop listening skills and explain meaning of the questions. These are good questions and hopefully will be discussed in class.
11:22	S. copies specific questions for the final test as the teacher dictates them.	Students copy questions.	Students are programmed to sit quietly and write.
11:28	S. leaves the room for a drink.	Students begin work on a character analysis.	Students have to wait for S. to return. A student is asked to read a character analysis aloud.
11:30	S. asks a question about completeness of character analysis. He states he has not started yet and laughs.	Students work on assignment.	Some students use this time to talk to each other.
11:33	S. takes out character analysis sheet and goes to teacher to ask question.	Teacher walks around the room and monitors work.	Most students are getting ready to leave class at bell.
11:35	S. works until bell rings.		
11:40	S. is standing talking quietly to other students.	Room is very cold and impersonal. No posters or decorations. Could be any class. Only 15 students.	S. is beginning to wonder why I am in all of his classes but does not ask.

Time	Specific behavior at 5-7 minute intervals	Environment	Impressions-Comments
11:42	S. sits quietly and looks at assignment that will be checked. Asks a question about assignment.	Students review assignments.	Papers are exchanged to be corrected. Teacher reads the answers very quickly.
11:45	S. receives a grade of 100 which he states proudly.	Students verbally give grades.	Some students are reluctant to relate poor grades.
11:50	S. gives a correct answer for a proportion question.	Students are attentive to the math explanation of proportion.	Explanation of the new concept is clear and well presented.
11:57	S. raises his hand to answer a problem from the book.	The class is busy doing problems for verbal answers.	The objective is to do sample problems and give verbal answers. S. is doing very well.
12:02	S. argues that if answers are apparent he should not have to do all steps in the problem solving. Is told he must do all steps on paper.	Students copy examples in notebooks as teacher does them on the board.	Teacher claims all steps are necessary on easy ones so they know the process for more difficult problems. This is accepted.
12:10	S. makes a trip to the pencil sharpener and wastebasket before beginning the homework assignment.	Class begins to work on assignment. Teacher sits at table correcting papers.	The teacher will help students if they come up to her and ask or go to them if they raise their hand.
12:17	S. is working diligently on his assignment.	The entire class is working quietly on assignment.	The teacher is walking around and appropriately monitoring students' work.
12:26	S. has stopped working and is looking around the class. He starts work again when I glance at him.	Class continues to work on the assignment.	Some students begin to watch the clock, rest their hand on their books, or just gaze into space. Too much time for seatwork. They are ready to go to lunch.
12:26	S. has quit work for the period. He is sitting quietly, daydreaming and waiting for the bell to ring.	Most of the class is just waiting for the dismissal bell.	The teacher is working with a student but rest of class is talking quietly.
12:36	S. went home for lunch.		
1:27	S. entered room and sat quietly in his seat. Talked with fellow students while waiting for the class to begin.	The room is a typical science room. Set-up for a lab situation.	There are 13 ninth grade students out of an enrollment of 29. The upper classmen are working on a science requirement.
1:32	S. opened lab books as instructed by the teacher.	The students were quiet and attentive at first but began talking as explanation continued.	The teacher reviewed the goals of the lab problem.

Time	Specific behavior at 5-7 minute intervals	Environment	Impression-Comments
1:39	S. began working on the lab problem when instructed to do so. Consulted with the student sitting next to him about the procedures.	Class began working on the lab problem. A number of them were off task.	The upper classmen were not very ready to begin working. The problem is supposed to take the whole period. I don't think it will.
1:43	S. is still trying to get started. Talks to neighbor and watches actions of other students.	Some students are fooling around as teacher moves around the room helping students and answering questions.	The students are not taking the lesson very seriously. They do not seem excited about epicenters of earthquakes.
1:46	S. raises hand for teacher help. Sits with hand up but gives up and lowers hand. Sits and talks to neighbor.	Students are talking and sharing answers.	Students are on task when teacher is near or is talking to them.
1:49	S. again raises hand for help. Gets help from teacher. Listens to explanation.	Most students are off task.	Students are getting answers from fellow classmates. Some are working together to solve lab problem.
1:55	S. raises hand for help. Lowers hand and copies from upper classman sitting next to him.	Many students socializing.	It is again apparent that class is only working on problem when teacher is nearby monitoring progress.
2:02-2:04	S. is on task and is now helping a friend with the problem. He seems to have discovered the purpose of the lab problem. He has reached a point where he again needs help and raises hand.	Some students have finished the lab and are just sitting and talking.	The class is coming to a close, so some who wasted time are getting worried that they won't finish. Many hands up for help.
2:06	S. finally gets to talk to the teacher.	Students begin to put away lab equipment.	Students who are not finished are walked through the process by the teacher.
2:10-2:18	S. is finished and hands in paper. Returns to seat and socializes quietly.	Class is mostly just sitting and talking.	This lab should not have taken the entire period. S. seems subdued.
2:22	S. arrives in the gym after changing. Begins to shoot baskets with teacher.	Comfortable, relaxed atmosphere. Teacher is shooting baskets with students.	S. is telling another student that I have been in every single class. I will interview him this period.
2:28	S. goes and sits down waiting for class to start.	Students listen to teacher tell them what they will be doing this period.	The class will be doing two activities. One group will test in apparatus and the other group will begin basketball unit.

Time	Specific behavior at 5-7 minute intervals	Environment	Impression-Comments
2:33	S. begins working on the basketball unit by shooting baskets from various parts of the floor. Is called to test on apparatus.	Students are practicing for tests or shooting baskets.	The students are interested and anxious for the activities to proceed.
2:37	S. is finished with the apparatus test and is shooting baskets from assigned spots on the floor.	Students on apparatus and working on test.	The class is obviously a culminating experience of an apparatus unit and an introduction to the basketball unit.
2:44	S. helps other students work on basketball. He tells other students which routine comes next.	Students working on apparatus or shooting baskets.	The class is working hard but students are interested and having a good time.
2:50	S. goes to change clothes for the interview.		

End-of-Day Interview

1. What do you like best about this school?

    I like sports the best, especially football. I like going home for lunch. I can pick more electives than in middle school. We have more freedom here.

2. What one thing would you change about the school if you could?

    I would change my starting time so I could get out earlier like last semester.

3. What is the best thing that happened to you in school today? This year?

    I got 100 in math class. I didn't flunk any classes. I got my career paper done.

4. What is the worst thing that happened to you in school today? This year?

    Going to typing class. I failed my semester final in astronomy. I got a "D−" in woodworking last semester. I want to be a carpenter so that's bad.

5. How would you describe this school to a newcomer?

    It is a good school. A lot of activities and sports. Nice teachers. This is a big school with a lot of kids. We have some good kids and some bad ones. Bad ones have drugs and are truant, but I don't know anything about the drugs. We have helpful guidance counselors. It has a good choice of electives. There is more freedom than the middle school and it's not as hard as I expected.

6. If you had a personal problem and wanted assistance is there someone here at school that you would readily turn to for advice?

    Yes. My guidance counselor. They care more than a teacher would. Not that a teacher wouldn't help but the counselor has more time.

Observer's Reactions

My first reaction was that I was tired. Tired of sitting, tired of writing, tired of listening to people talk. I was mentally and physically tired. I wondered if I could be a ninth grader five days a week, 180 days a year.

My main impression was the absence of any form of individualization of material. All students were on the same page, doing the same activities, listening to the same information. A gifted student would be bored and a slow student would easily fall behind. It is possible that teachers allow for such differences when evaluating work, but I do not know this to be true.

I was amazed at the amount of copying in notebooks that was expected. The teacher would dictate and the student would write the dictation verbatim. Why couldn't the material be mimeographed and distributed? This would provide time for teaching.

I was impressed by the clarity of some instructions that were provided by some teachers. This was, in many instances, well done.

The classrooms were sterile and cold in atmosphere. To be fair, many teachers share the same room so ownership of a room doesn't exist. The desks were in rows and students sat in rows. The students were well behaved and surprisingly attentive. I could have fallen asleep on a couple of occasions.

With the exception of a few bright spots, it was a mind deadening day. I would not want to be a ninth grader again. This is in no way an indictment of the good school or the good teachers I observed. An observation of one day in no way tells the whole story or gives a complete picture. Some of the classes were wrapping up units prior to the end of the quarter, and review is never as interesting as the initial presentation would or could be.

The students felt very secure and there was a safe, relaxed atmosphere in the whole school. Neither students nor teachers were uptight or apprehensive. I felt very comfortable in the halls between classes and in the cafeteria. The students either ignored me or were friendly. It was apparent that a lot of work had gone into making this relaxed environment.

The students were polite, attentive, and well behaved in most classes. They were serious about their work and tried to be successful.

This experience was a real eye-opener as far as what it is like to be a ninth grader. I am glad I participated in the project, and I hope the results will lead to an improved educational program for many students.

Shadow Study Number 2

Conducted in a suburban high school, grades 9-12, which enrolled in excess of 1,600 students. The 15-year-old student was above average.

Time	Specific behavior at 5-7 minute intervals	Environment	Impression-Comments
Period I English 9 Core II			
7:45	Seated quietly ahead of time for class. On task.	Five rows, 6 chairs each.	Teacher referred to class as a difficult group. "Don't want you writing in dictionaries or throwing them around the room."
7:50	"Sailed" a copy of worksheet to other student in his row—went out of his way to help, then went to teacher's desk to work.	Students working in pairs or small groups—some commotion. Twenty-five students in class but it seemed like many more.	Tough social environment. "This guy's (to me) gotta' be a senior."
7:57	Seated in own seat working on worksheet with dictionary and student seated behind him.	Everyone pretty much on task (worksheet). Hum of conversation.	I have a feeling that my presence has had a dampening effect on some members of this class. This is reality.

Time	Specific behavior at 5-7 minute intervals	Environment	Impression-Comments
8:04	Seated, looking into space with chin resting on his propped up hand.	Everyone pretty much on task (worksheet). Hum of conversation.	Blinds drawn to avoid distraction of passing train. Strongly suspect one girl is high.
8:11	Reading in dictionary—fiddling with pencil.	Someone evidently tossed a dictionary.	Hope I don't have to make a bathroom stop.
8:18	Watching as his teacher works with student next to him—still on worksheet.	Fairly high level of conversation in the room.	It would be fairly easy to get distracted.
8:25	Chewing on his finger—looking at a folded sheet.	Students working on worksheet.	"Nobody else is playing and you can't hear him play his saxophone."
8:32	R. is gone (he does attendance for the office at the end of class).		Class has about 6 tough discipline problems, another 8 who support them—left about 11 on task.

Period II Typing

Time	Specific behavior at 5-7 minute intervals	Environment	Impression-Comments
8:40	R. is seated in typing class and listening to the principal doing a.m. announcements.	Thirty-eight typewriters in a spacious business ed room—one drape closed—two open—only 12 students in class.	Teacher was surprised to learn that she had a ninth grader in this typing class.
8:47	R. is seated at his typewriter while teacher is going over a grammar exercise.	Everyone on task and down to business.	Amazing to find verb agreement, pronoun antecedent, and punctuation exercises; punctuation error.
8:54	Working on a time accuracy exercise in typing.		
9:00	Still working on time test.		
9:07	Still working on time typing assignment.		
9:14	Still working on time typing assignment.	Everyone still on task.	What a contrast with last hour—a dozen students and no visible discipline problems—upper classmen not plagued with identity confusion of earlier class (i.e., delinquency vs. responsibility).
9:21	Working on new typing exercise (drill sheet).	Everyone still on task.	
9:28	Working on new typing exercise (drill sheet).	Everyone still on task.	

Time	Specific behavior at 5-7 minute intervals	Environment	Impression-Comments
9:33	Finishing up work to hand in at end of hour.		It was reminiscent of the "old days" to see all classes changing at the same time and students going to all parts of the building.

Period III Science

Time	Specific behavior at 5-7 minute intervals	Environment	Impression-Comments
9:39	Sitting in science class visiting quietly with student next to him (his shirt is ripped in the right armpit).	Kids are in class visiting with one another and asking questions of teacher.	Teacher looking forward to lesson—"too many for science class (28)" wearing shirt and tie—19 girls, 9 boys. (Room size and facilities don't compare with ours even though this is a senior high.)
9:46	Chewing on finger and staring at blackboard.	Teacher is introducing a sludge lab and asking clarifying questions.	
9:52	Rubbing his finger on table top, listening to teacher's directions for lab—yawning.	Teacher giving very clear directions and written outline.	
9:59	Listening to instructions for lab.	Teacher giving very clear directions and written outline.	Kids were fascinated with their "sludge."
10:06	Intently examining his sludge and sharing observations about it with his lab partner.	Kids moving freely about the room, working with a variety of equipment, and staying productively engaged.	Responses to "sludge" were typically early adolescent— enthusiastic, clowning, performing for one another.
10:12	Apply flammability test to sludge with sensational results—he lit strip that his partner held.		
10:19	Writing observation notes in his notebook and intently studying sludge comments with partner.	Everyone on task.	
10:26	Clean-up time in lab—delivering sludge to front desk—patiently waits his turn.	Excitement of moving to next class picking up.	Boys and girls pretty much separated. Nearly all the boys and nearly all the girls are in jeans—mostly red tag Levis.

Period IV Algebra II

Time	Specific behavior at 5-7 minute intervals	Environment	Impression-Comments
10:35	Seated in algebra class listening to teacher.	Algebra classroom shades drawn—teacher going over test.	Twenty-four students. Work is a very effective means of control. Math works well because expectations and process are both clear.

32

Time	Specific behavior at 5-7 minute intervals	Environment	Impression-Comments
10:42	Listening to teacher, fiddling with papers and pages in book (quietly).	Relaxed atmosphere, one question volunteered in first 10 minutes.	
10:50	Watching teacher work out a word problem.	Nearly everyone appears to be on task—three or four students volunteering information.	Teacher using white paper and magic marker over blackboard.
10:56	Chewing on pen and listening to teacher.	Class sitting quietly.	"Betcha' can't figure it out." Good challenging comment. Good use of calculator—intent on problem format, not calculation. "Use your calculator for that."
11:02	Listening to teacher's presentation—studying problem in book.	Class sitting quietly dealing with fairly abstract topic.	
11:09	Seated—listening to teacher's explanation and following along in book.	Class sitting quietly dealing with fairly abstract topic.	Excellent pace—leaves time for thought.
11:16	Looking down at book and watching teacher intermittently.	Class struggling with the notion of a constant.	Got very complicated at end.
11:22	Writing on his paper working from text.	Teacher trying to explain "constant."	Where's a bathroom? How does the lunchroom work?
11:30	Lunch and open period. R. seemed to enjoy lunch and a chance to visit with his friends.	Lunchroom was spacious and pleasant—friendly but *assertive* monitor.	Monitor felt that ninth graders keep very much to themselves except for the kids who are "hard to manage." They are accepted by "hard to manage" senior high kids.

Period V Computer

Time	Specific behavior at 5-7 minute intervals	Environment	Impression-Comments
12:35	Student came to class early and started working with micro—seems interested in learning.	Computer lab—15 micros, plenty of space. Apple IIe lab; most have two disk drives. Two students work at each micro.	Class seemed to be self-starting. Lots of interest and independent work. Designed to familiarize kids with basics of programming.
12:45	Partner is on machine while R. is watching and offering suggestions.	Good work environment—kids work uninhibited but engaged.	I was disturbed to hear a fair amount of "bad" language. Evidently it comes quite naturally to kids this age.
12:55	Partner is on machine while R. is watching and offering suggestions.		

Time	Specific behavior at 5-7 minute intervals	Environment	Impression-Comments
12:59	Engaged in a spirited discussion trying to get lab partner through a command on micro.		I suspect this class represents the most dramatic difference in the past 10 years curriculum-wise.
1:07	Still observer while partner works at terminal—discussing the work.		These lab stools are really hard on the back, neck, and shoulders.
1:13	Loading a new disk into the micro—he hasn't got to the controls.		
1:20	Loading a new disk into the micro—he still hasn't got to the controls.		

Period VI Civics

Time	Specific behavior at 5-7 minute intervals	Environment	Impression-Comments
1:28	Arrived early to his last hour class and took his own seat and stayed there.	Lots of informal talk in the classroom—kidding between teacher and kids.	By the end of the day, the kids' curiosity was too much for them. "Why are you following us?"
1:35	Class getting underway—sitting quietly.	Class is fairly open and spirited; students *not* always on task.	
1:42	Talking with two other boys about something that another student had demonstrated.		Kids seem to reveal more immature behavior.
1:49	Folding a sheet of paper lengthwise to use in Johari's Window exercise—on task.	Class is pretty much into the assignment.	This should be a very good exercise for R.
1:55	Throwing an elbow into the air in front of him as he finished his list of opinions about himself.	One student shouted loudly. Teacher ignored him, class handled it okay.	Attention seeking—same this a.m.
2:01	Chewing on his thumb finishing off his list of opinions.	Some students completing assignment—"I'm done, I'm done."	Hard to deal with attention seeking behavior. Kids generally working quietly and independently. Sitting in a circle would have helped.
2:06	Leaning his cheek on his propped up hand and leafing through papers.	Students and teacher carrying on a discussion—film next door makes it hard for me to hear.	R. doesn't appear to be a contributor to class. He seems to observe and listen but to be otherwise detached.
2:12	Chewing on finger—shifting in his chair.	Students talking—they go to the edge of rowdy and then recede.	Short assignment—trying to convince the class that the assignment is reasonable. "Absolutely quiet during the few minutes left."

34

Time	Specific behavior at 5-7 minute intervals	Environment	Impression-Comments
2:18	Sitting quietly and writing in his notebook.	Most students are quietly working on reading assignment.	I'm beat.

End-of-Day Interview

1. What do you like best about this school?

    Different classes, variety of classes.

2. What one thing would you change about the school if you could?

    Nothing.

3. What is the best thing that happened to you in school today? This year?

    Computer time.

    Getting good teachers.

4. What is the worst thing that happened to you in school today? This year?

    Shadow made me nervous.

    My locker falling apart.

5. How would you describe this school to a newcomer?

    Confusing to find your way around.

6. If you had a personal problem and wanted assistance is there someone here at school that you would readily turn to for advice?

    Counselor—can't remember name.

Observer's Reactions

Having spent a day observing a ninth grade student, some of my reactions, feelings, and judgments are:

I was again reminded of *how much students have to give up in order to get an education.* My entire day was spent sitting. Most of the time, except for part of science class and for the computer lab, I was in one of five or six rows with five or six chairs in each row. I had to worry about finding my way around the building, finding a bathroom, squeezing in a hasty lunch in a *large* lunchroom (seats 600+), and taking notes all day long.

I had to submit to someone else's plan for my time for 6½ hours. I missed my friends. At the end of the day I went to my next meeting exhausted. My student was looking forward to going to the computer lab—where the highlight of his day could be realized—actually getting some "hands on" computer time.

The 9-12 setting was quite different from our school—so many more kids and the ninth graders were the small ones. Most of the ninth grade classes were similar to those in our 7-9 arrangement. The typing class was the exception: That was mostly made up of upperclassmen, and the teacher was truly all "business." Very adult-oriented as contrasted with the orientation of a typical middle-level teacher.

The lunchroom supervisor was not enthusiastic about having the ninth graders. She felt like the immature kids were patsies for some of the tougher upper classmen.

I was especially interested to hear R. say that he appreciated the "variety" in his schedule when in reality he sat all day long. He had no activity, or practical arts, or drama, or 35 journalism, etc., in his schedule. I concluded that he really likes the computer and that's what he meant by variety.

R. is slightly below average in height and a little on the heavy side. He looks like some of that baby fat is still "hanging around" him—literally. He is generally quiet and seems fairly committed to school. It could be that he relates more "intimately" to school than he does to other kids.

He is one of those guys who appears to be asexual—*no* connections with the girls in his school, and not many close connections with boys other than as classes "throw" them together (e.g., in computer lab and science and to a lesser degree in English). This is a good reminder to use schools for that purpose.

His comments fit my observations of him. He likes the variety of classes, everything is fine, I made him nervous, the school has "pretty good" teachers but the building is confusing. He said he would go to a counselor but couldn't give the person's name—said he knew where to look it up.

When you put this together with his tendency to come early to class, to pick up attendance slips, to want to please adults in general, and his wearing of the only pair of grey cords I saw all day (nearly everyone wore jeans—most Levi red tags), you have evidence which suggests that R. is not the social leader of his grade.

Teachers referred to him as a nice or good kid, but no one sought him out nor did any teacher call on him during the entire day. His nonverbal behavior suggested that he was comfortable and didn't expect to contribute in class or to be called upon.

Shadow Study Number 3

Conducted in a suburban high school of 700 pupils in grades 9-12. This able student had just turned 15.

Time	Specific behavior at 5-7 minute intervals	Environment	Impression-Comments
7:30	Becky wrote letter or note on lined loose-leaf paper in ink.	Homeroom period. Twenty-one males and females—all ninth grade. Room usually used to teach languages. Many colorful posters. Written on board: "*Last Day* for all *Make-Ups* Thursday March 8," followed by list of 12 students. Classroom is large, light, and spacious. Walls are yellow. Florescent lighting—all light operating well.	Students talk quietly while announcements are being broadcast over the public address system. Teacher with quiet voice and pleasant tone said, "Ssh. Let's be quiet." Students continue to converse quietly with each other.
7:37	Becky goes to locker to get study materials to be used while juniors and seniors attend an assembly.		
7:40	Becky returned with loose-leaf notebook and with one small paperback book.		
7:45	A girl student two rows over from Becky calls to Becky with a comment about a reading assignment. Becky responds, "Don't worry about it. It's wicked good."	Papers rattle. Pages turn. Quiet talking. Teacher is busy at her desk in front of the room.	Two boys talking in back corner of the room. Teacher: "Ssh." Talking continues more quietly and then stops.

Time	Specific behavior at 5-7 minute intervals	Environment	Impression-Comments
7:50	Becky is studying history text and writing a penciled report.	Sound of blower of hot air system. Sound of lockers in hall opening and closing. Still some quiet conversation.	
7:55	Becky still reading history text and adding to a written report.	A teacher who shares use of the classroom enters leaving door open. Increased noise from hallway outside of classroom.	
8:00	Becky still bent over book and writing.	Assistant principal's voice comes over public address system requesting to see a number of students. His voice is courteous, calm, and matter-of-fact.	Two new voices join those quietly talking.
8:03	Bell rings. The student who asked Becky about the reading assignment calls to Becky, "That book is good." Becky answers, "I told you it is. Ellen, wait up."		
8:08	Natural science class. Becky is sitting in seat near front of room watching the teacher who is standing in front of the class demonstrating some principles about the workings of simple machines. Becky's elbow rests on her desk and her chin rests on her hand.	This is a ninth grade class. A student sneezes and several students say, "Bless you." The teacher combines a lecture with many illustrations and examples written on the blackboard plus lots of questions addressed to the class as a whole. Students sometimes raise hands to respond and sometimes just respond.	Interspersed with the lecture and demonstrations the teacher offers much positive support and some humor. He says, "I was so proud of you on your quizzes. There was not anyone who did not have the units down right." The classroom atmosphere seems very comfortable emotionally and focused on helping the students understand that $F_1 \times D_1 = F_2 \times D_2$. All students seem attentive.
8:15	Becky shifts to resting the other elbow on her desk and rests her chin on her hand.	This is a science laboratory classroom. Several sinks and 12 tables four feet apart, two students seated at table plus one row of desks in the back row composed of pairs of student desks pushed together to correspond with the rows of tables.	
8:20	Becky and other students are working at their seats on a problem the teacher has written on the blackboard.	The students ask many questions while the teacher is working out the problem on the blackboard.	At this point a bell rings, and students gather their belongings and prepare to leave the classroom. Teacher telephones the office to verify that bell sounded in error.

Time	Specific behavior at 5-7 minute intervals	Environment	Impression-Comments
8:20	Becky laughs in response to the bell incident.	Teacher puts another sample problem on the blackboard.	Students try to work out problem in their notebooks and continue to ask many questions to which teacher responds with clarity and good humor.
8:25	Becky is working on problem in her notebook.		
8:30	Becky yawns. She continues to watch the teacher and seems to be listening attentively.	Another bell rings in error. Teacher continues to demonstrate the same principle by writing another problem on the blackboard.	
8:35	Becky is sitting back in her chair watching the teacher at the blackboard. Becky's arms are folded across her chest.	The teacher is explaining how the arm is a fulcrum. He illustrates how power is sacrificed for speed and distance using hockey sticks, knives, and baseball bats as examples.	While the teacher is erasing board he comments about teacher X who, he says, does not use an eraser but throws himself against the blackboard. Students laugh. Work goes on.
8:42	Becky still watching the teacher and seems to be listening. She leans back in the chair again and folds her arms.	Students are preparing to leave. Teacher continues to teach.	Assignment is to look at home for simple machines that are taken for granted and used every day. Diagrams the machine and measures the F_1 and F_2. The more unique the choice, the more extra points the student will earn.
8:47	Algebra I class. Becky takes out her homework and reviews it.	Again she sits in front of the classroom. The teacher has a "machine gun" delivery of explanations.	The teacher begins the class by announcing that midquarter warnings are due today and students can line up alphabetically because there is one for everyone. Students laugh. Included with explanations of problems were comments such as "You people did not do well on your last quiz," "Yesterday's silly mistakes," "There is no point in ploughing ahead and running into a wall," "You should pay a little more attention," "You did a lot of fouling up on those," etc.
8:52	Becky listens and notes as teacher explains factoring, canceling, etc.	Students are quiet and seem very serious.	

38

Time	Specific behavior at 5-7 minute intervals	Environment	Impression-Comments
9:02	Becky is watching and listening.	One student sighs loudly.	
9:07	Becky is working at her desk solving problems written on the board.		
9:13	Becky is watching teacher at the board, leaning on her elbow. She has stopped working out the problems in her notebook.		
9:21	Still watching. Hand on cheek. Elbow on knee.		Offers of help included "It's your grade, kid. Ask if you have a question." "Don't just stick to division. Are there any other problems that bother you?" Students talk to each other while the list is being read. The teacher tried some jokes that did not quite make it and one student responded humorlessly, "Ha ha."
9:25	Book closed. Arms folded across chest. Foot tapping.	Using public address system, assistant principal calls a list of 19 students to go to the office.	
9:30	Becky looks bored. Bell rings.	As Becky exits to hall, several girl friends approach her and they talk.	
9:38	Ninth grade English class.	The class is studying *Great Expectations.* Apparently the teacher had given the students questions to be answered as they read the assignment. The teacher read some of the book, then the question students had been given, and then a student was named to answer the question. Often the teacher would name the page on which the answer could be found.	The teacher gives positive response to incorrect answers, i.e., "Yes and even more than that. . . ."
9:42	Becky is tapping her foot and watching the teacher. Again, Becky is sitting in the front of the classroom. The teacher repeats the question, and rephrases it. Becky answers the question.		
9:50	Becky is copying a list of adjectives as suggested to the class by the teacher.		

Time	Specific behavior at 5-7 minute intervals	Environment	Impression-Comments
9:55	Becky's head is bent over her book. She may be asleep. She lifts her head and rubs her eyes.	A student is reading a passage aloud. He reads poorly and other students laugh. The boy laughs also.	
10:00	The teacher calls on Becky again. Becky says "I didn't read this yet." "That's right," said the teacher, "that's for tomorrow."		
10:07	Becky yawns and stretches.	The teacher shifts to preparing the class for grammar and mechanics test to be given Friday to determine level of placement in English classes in tenth grade. A grammar exercise is assigned. Adverbial subordinate clauses are reviewed.	
10:12	Becky gets up and gets a dictionary from the window sill. She returns to her seat and works on the history report she had written during the homeroom period.	Other students are watching the teacher, who is writing sentences on the blackboard. The students listen to the teacher's explanations and ask questions.	
10:20	World history class. Becky continues to write her report.	Much conversation among students. The teacher is checking each student's homework and marks in her classbook as she makes comments about the student's report. The suggestions begin, "All right, but I want to see more," or, "You might find it easier if you. . . . ," or, "If you get a chance. . . ."	
10:20	To Becky the teacher said, "This is okay for an essay, but for our purpose you might want to split it up into two paragraphs."		
10:25	The pencilled report is on Becky's desk and Becky is attentive now and watching the teacher.		The teacher is asking questions that require analytical thought. "How are King Alfred and Charlemagne alike?" "In what ways are they different?"
10:30	Becky volunteers an answer. She has some difficulty expressing herself but manages okay.		The teacher responds "That's a good point. It is a good thing to have your opinion."

40

Time	Specific behavior at 5-7 minute intervals	Environment	Impression-Comments
10:35	Becky is the first student to laugh when the teacher asks for a volunteer to read a certain passage. The teacher asks why and Becky says, "That is written in Old English."		
10:40	Becky is smiling and crumpling the corners of pages in her history book.	Teacher reassures a student, "Your opinion is as good as Karen's." Lively discussion about whether Alfred's desire to leave a memory of himself was bad.	
10:45	Becky looks attentively at a student who is defending a position.		
10:48	Becky yawns and stretches.	Discussion of meaning of Chronicles.	
10:53	Becky volunteered answer to similarity between methods of Charlemagne and Alfred.		
10:57	Becky stopped at teacher's desk on her way out of the classroom. Becky then joined two friends and left the classroom.	Bell rang and assignment made.	
11:11	Ninth grade coeducational physical education class. Becky is the last of the group to be seated when the male teacher insists that all sit down to hear announcements.	This is the day to switch phys. ed. activities. A male and a female teacher are in charge. He quiets the assembled group and the female teacher announces that the new choices will be street hockey or badminton.	
11:16	Becky selected street hockey as her activity, indicated by the fact she jumped up smiling and ran to the adjacent gymnasium, literally bounding.		
11:22	Becky climbed to the top of the unfolded bleachers to watch the first set of players. She cheered and encouraged players.		

41

Time	Specific behavior at 5-7 minute intervals	Environment	Impression-Comments
11:28	Becky changed places with a member of the "red" team. She followed the other team members and watched the actions, cheering when the red team scored. She jumped from the top of the bleachers to enter the game.	The male teacher watched and announced when it was time for a new set of players to enter the game. There was positive support from him and no corrections or suggestions were made of anyone's participation.	
11:33	Becky returned to the top of the bleachers giving her hockey stick to a girlfriend who entered the game. She laughed and talked with her girlfriends while the play continued.		
11:38	Becky still sitting at top of the bleachers. She is very animated, laughing loudly, pointing at a friend sitting near her, talking and moving around a great deal.		
11:44	Becky is back in the game. This time she is holding the stick by the wrong end. Suddenly a student assistant, a star goalie on the high school hockey team, takes goalie position. Becky gets serious about playing and enthusiastically makes several shots. Some are very good and some miss.		
11:49	She goes to the girls' locker room to change.		
11:59	Becky is eating lunch purchased in the school cafeteria, sitting at a table with ninth grade girls and senior girls. She and her friends seem to be having a good time —much talk and laughter.	Approximately 200 students are eating in the cafeteria. The assistant principal and a teacher are present.	
12:03	Becky still at the lunch table, eating ice cream and talking with friends. Now she is listening to a girlfriend rather thoughtfully, head-nodding, etc.		
12:12	Standing in lobby outside of cafeteria talking with friends.	Many students in the same location waiting for bell to ring to indicate time to go to sixth period class. Lots of talking and moving around and positive energy.	

42

Time	Specific behavior at 5-7 minute intervals	Environment	Impression-Comments
12:16	First year typing class. Becky takes paper from a wire basket on the teacher's desk.	All students busy themselves at a typewriter soon after they enter the class. They seem to know what to do. Some typewriters are out of service and teacher is assisting student to find another seat where a typewriter is available.	
12:21	Becky is doing a warm-up typing exercise.		
12:26	Becky is listening to teacher who is instructing (really reviewing) class about proper procedures used in writing business letters.	The room is quiet and all students are attentive. The pace of questions is brisk. Teacher asks and students respond. Teacher invites student questions, and answers them courteously, completely, and pleasantly.	
12:33	Becky is studying her typing text and proceeds slowly to type.		
12:38	Becky finishes the assigned letter before many and after some other students, and takes the letter to the teacher to be checked, as do the other students.	The teacher uses a chart on the board to help students determine the letter grade represented by their words per minute in combination with their errors.	
12:41	Becky has completed an envelope for her letter and is talking with the girl behind her.		
12:46	Becky is working on a typing assignment to type a certain passage until the student completes three lines without an error.		This assignment is introduced by the teacher asking, "Can you do three lines in one minute with no errors. How many think they can?
12:50	Becky is taking a one minute timing.		
12:55	Becky crumples her paper and throws it in the wastebasket just before the teacher asks that the papers be handed in. She looks embarrassed and removes the paper from the wastebasket, smooths it and places it in a wire basket on the teacher's desk.		

Time	Specific behavior at 5-7 minute intervals	Environment	Impression-Comments
1:03	Spanish I class	This class is taught by Becky's homeroom teacher in the same room in which Becky attends homeroom.	
	Becky is asked to write a sentence from the assigned homework on the board. She rises quickly to her feet and hurries to the board where the job is done very quickly and seemingly confidently.	Several students are selected to write sentences from homework assignment on the blackboard. They go quickly and willingly and look at each other's completed sentence. One student speaks quietly to the girl writing beside her, and the second girl erases a word ending and writes in another one.	
1:08	Becky is standing near the sentence on the board and the teacher is checking each sentence. Becky's sentence is declared "Perfecto" and Becky looks pleased.	The teacher gives much positive support in both word and gestures, i.e., "Perfecto," "muy bien," and "excellente."	
1:12	Becky helps a late arriving classmate to find the place in the book.		
1:17	The teacher is asking many questions in Spanish and students are answering when the teacher calls their name. Becky seems very attentive.		
1:20	The teacher has instructed the class in Spanish and Becky seems to be looking through her notebook for a paper. At this point I explain to Becky and to the class the nature of my mission there and leave the class with Becky to interview her.		

End-of-Day Interview

1. What do you like best about this school?

   The people in my classes.

2. What one thing about the school would you change if you could?

   Long pause followed by "I really can't think of anything I would change."

3. What is the best thing that happened to you in school today? This year?

   Eating lunch. I had had no breakfast and was really hungry.

I've made a lot of new friends and have a lot of new people in my classes. I have a lot more fun now. Last year I was in all honors classes. I applied for four honors classes this year—science, history, English,and Spanish. I only got honors history.

4. What is the worst thing that happened to you in school today? This year?

Feeling weird because I was wondering if I was being followed. I got in bed late last night because I got behind in history and had to read three chapters to catch up.

Being separated from my friends. I hardly ever see them.

5. How would you describe this school to a newcomer?

Our days are slow compared with the schools in X (the next town). That's because that school is bigger and the classes are farther apart.

6. If you had a personal problem and wanted assistance, is there someone here at school that you would readily turn to for advice?

Yes, I would talk to Ella about it. She used to be my best friend and then we weren't friends for a while, but now we're best friends again.

Observer's Reactions

This experience impresses me again with how much the style and attitude of the teacher shape the learning experience for the students. I was impressed with the tenacity with which Becky attended to her class instruction throughout the day. Becky seemed so much more responsive in class situations that sought student response and student opinions, i.e., the science class that used for demonstration objects familiar to the students, and the history class that encouraged student opinions about issues.

I was interested in Becky's style in various situations of being almost tentative in her first response—in history when answering questions, and in physical education in particular. Becky explained during our interview that she was more tired than usual on this day because she had studied late the night before. I certainly noted the passivity and withdrawal in the math class as compared with her attentiveness in other situations.

I find I am thinking a lot about Becky's feelings about her class assignments this year. She was moved from the honors program in several areas to regular college preparatory classes. This move seemed to have severe social consequences. Many friends were lost, new ones were gained, and just recently some were regained. Obviously, Becky has developed respect for her new classmates and said that she finds them more interesting and more fun than the ones in her honors classes.

The day was a most valuable experience, although I was much more tired than usual at the end of the school day.

Perhaps you would be interested in the reaction of Becky and of other students to the process of this study. The students seemed to accept my presence with no difficulty. Two students asked what I was doing and seemed satisfied when I said that I was taking part in a research study. I did not know Becky at all before this shadowing experience. She said later that she became uneasy and wondered if I could be following her at the beginning of the fifth class period.

During our end-of-the-day interview I gave her a copy of the first three paragraphs of the sheet entitled HOW FARES THE NINTH GRADE/OVERVIEW. She seemed to understand the nature of the study, and I was able to give her some positive feedback about her helpfulness to other students, her leadership among her friends, and her obvious attentiveness and courtesy in classes.

I contacted the teachers on the day before the study to explain my presence in their classes. They were most cooperative and seemed comfortable.

I enjoyed very much participating in this study and certainly look forward to reading about the results.

Shadow Study Number 4

Conducted in a small-town junior high school which enrolls 900 pupils in grades 8-9. The student was 15 years old and was considered average in ability.

Time	Specific behavior at 5-7 minute intervals	Environment	Impressions-Comments
8:20	T. sitting quietly, head in hand, jeans and a jacket (which is practically the uniform). Homeroom doesn't start for five minutes.	Typical classroom—five rows of six chairs each. Room clean and fairly attractive.	Practically everybody in seat way ahead of time, quiet conversation and socialization ongoing.
8:25	Oral roll call—Sitting quietly.	Classroom rules posted—room used for English and Spanish classes.	
8:30	T. in conversation with peers.	Announcements over P.A. by principal.	
8:35	Same—until passing bell rang, then got up and went into hall—even though first class was here.		
8:42	Took seat, opened book (notebook). This is an elective Spanish I class—24 students.	Students still coming in—homework being collected and/or checked in notebooks by teacher.	
8:50	T. checking over his test which had just been returned (apparently graded by teacher last night).	Teacher spoke in Spanish much of time.	Class very orderly. Typical class, Q & A, lots of volunteers to respond and write on board.
8:57	Looking at board and his paper to check against sentences that had been placed on board. T. quiet but following lesson.	Same.	Grammar seemed to be emphasized as much as pronunciation.
9:03	T. at board, writing Spanish phrase, along with six other volunteers.	Same.	
9:09	Spoke aloud in both Spanish and English giving his phrase—smiled.	Same.	
9:17	Whole class, including T., speaking aloud in Spanish using material on board.		
9:23	Participating with whole class in reading aloud in Spanish from textbook.	Good atmosphere.	All students seem to be participating.

Time	Specific behavior at 5-7 minute intervals	Environment	Impression-Comments
9:30	T. listening to teacher reviewing some specific points.		Assignment given—write original sentences using 15 new words.
9:40	T. locating place in notebook where last lesson left off—as is rest of class.	Now in another building. Science lab tables and chairs—21 students—roll called.	Class slow to settle in— teacher seemed uncertain of where to start.
9:46	Entering notes given by teacher in his notebook.		Teacher related lesson to this state and tried to use examples.
9:52	Comparing notes with student next to him.		
10:00	Listening to teacher explaining three types of rocks.		
10:07	Same.		Did a brief demonstration with rocks in water.
10:12	Same.		
10:19	Waiting for test paper to be returned (two students passing them out).	Class mind disintegrated, not now together.	
10:25	Copying assignment in notebook as teacher explains it and puts it on board.	Class has, for all practical purposes, ended.	Chapter 10, selected questions, is assignment.
10:30	Looking at magazine with student next to him while waiting for bell.		
10:36	T. writing in notebook while other students are responding.	Literature class in portable classroom.	Teacher called class down several times asking for quiet.
10:42	Seems out of it at the moment. Teacher in conversation with a few students.	Lots of Panama Jack shirts in evidence.	
10:50	T. is one of five students standing around teacher to have their notebooks checked.	Teacher helping individuals —checking notebooks, recording grades.	
10:56	Reading silently from literature text (as others are).		
11:02	Same.		
11:08	Same.		Some students got passes to go to library and get a book for reports.

Time	Specific behavior at 5-7 minute intervals	Environment	Impression-Comments
11:15	Same—some students now into other things.	Two students reading "Dear Abby" in local paper—asked teacher meaning of "liaison."	
11:23	T. has stacked books and is waiting for bell.		
11:30	T. talking quietly with girl in front of him.	Algebra I class—29 students.	Tomorrow state-wide test (CRT) will be given.
11:36	T. has hand raised volunteering to put problem on board (didn't get selected this time—but did next time).		
11:42	T. having some problem with his problem at board—others have finished. Teacher prompts him and he worked factoring out.		Practically all students took a turn at board.
11:50	Laughing with others at a class character.	Lunch period built into this class—20 minutes.	
12:05	Eating lunch down table from me—during lunch voluntary segregation seemed to re-occur as it was during HR. Class seating patterns quite integrated.		
12:15	Same.		
12:32	Working problems at his desk and on his own.	Class settled back to work problem. Teacher had put on board.	Teacher moved about giving individual help.
12:38	Finished—thumbing through book and looking around—sorta waiting.		
12:46	Same.	Teacher had to request quiet.	
12:52	At another student's desk discussing a problem—he had gotten up.		
1:10	Seated—waiting for rest.	Band room—crowded, hard to get everybody in and ready with instruments. Roll called.	T. is now very aware of my continued presence—makes eye contact—we spoke briefly at lunch and beginning of this class.
1:17	Seated, minding his own business, book in lap—no instrument.		
1:23	Seated, minding his own business, book in lap—no instrument.	T. obviously is not participating with others—no instrument. I'll inquire why.	

Time	Specific behavior at 5-7 minute intervals	Environment	Impression-Comments
1:30	Seated, minding his own business, book in lap—no instrument.		
1:37	Seated, minding his own business, book in lap—no instrument.		
1:45	Seated, minding his own business, book in lap—no instrument.		At end of class I spoke to teacher. She showed me note requesting T. be excused from playing. Had left saxophone at grandmother's—also going to doctor after school—respiratory problem.

Twenty minute break—sun out but cool—most students stayed inside. I discovered regular teacher for last period is out sick.

Time	Specific behavior	Environment	Impression-Comments
2:20	Student teacher and substitute present. Students were asked to read Chapter II and write out answers to questions to be turned in tomorow.	Portable classroom—Social studies—Free enterprise.	A number of kids spoke with me as they, by now, had become comfortable with me—one sold me a nut bar—project of Latin Club.
2:27	Same.	Everybody at work.	
2:33	Same.		

2:35 Since nothing happened I took T. out so I could interview him. Had cleared this with teacher ahead of time. We went to counselor's office for interview.

3:10 School dismissed.

End-of-Day Interview

1. What do you like best about this school?

   Teachers, I really like them, can relate to them. They have enough time to help everybody.

2. What one thing would you change about the school if you could?

   Longer class periods (surprising since they are 55 minutes).

3. What is the best thing that happened to you in school today? This year?

   Nothing today. For the year "the State Beta Club Convention."

4. What is the worst thing that happened to you in school today? This year?

   Nothing today. For the year, I had worked hard on a book report but didn't get the grade I had worked for.

5. How would you describe this school to a newcomer?

   A place where you can have fun while learning—the teachers are good.

6. If you had a personal problem and wanted assistance is there someone here at school that you would readily turn to for advice?

   Yes, the teachers.

Observer's Reactions

Having spent a day observing a ninth grade student, some of my reactions, feelings, and judgments are:

I have mixed feelings. Overall discipline was good, students were not disrespectful or rowdy (with a couple of normal exceptions). Races interacted with no evident tension (student body is majority black). Teachers were conscientious and helpful to individuals. It was a very typical school day.

But—something was missing, it seemed. There was very little engagement or involvement with emotion. The content was exclusively from textbooks, and the lessons smacked of being just academic exercises. An awful lot of wasted time and waiting time was evident, while engaged learning time was limited.

Board work and seatwork were common while direct instruction was infrequent. Correctness and conformity were evident objectives while creativity and critical thinking did not seem to be called for.

Nothing during the day seemed to relate in any way to any of the developmental tasks of adolescence, or to 1984 (let alone March, 1984). Could well have been my own ninth grade *circa* 1934, 50 years ago, both in content and procedures. Classes were completely independent of one another with no evidence of interdepartmental planning apparent.

Shadow Study Number 5

Conducted in a 7-9 junior high school of 600 pupils located in a suburban area. The student, who had turned 15 a month before, was judged to be above average in academic ability.

Time	Specific behavior at 5-7 minute intervals	Environment	Impressions-Comments
French 9:05	Checking homework. J. asks teacher question—laughs when another student answers wrong. Slumped over his desk chewing on fingernail.	Regular classroom—sunny day. Displays of student work on walls. Cheerful atmosphere.	Small class (French) 12 students. Rest on field trip. Relaxed, casual.
9:10	J. answers a question with some difficulty. Laughs with student next to him. Nervous laugh. Biting on his pen. Conversing with neighbor about next homework question.	Teacher is still reviewing homework assignment. Quiet—calm morning.	No one concerned with my presence. Students relatively passive. Teacher dominating.
9:18	J. is a little jittery as the teacher reads a French passage. His notebook is sloppy and falling apart as he pages through it trying in vain to organize the papers.	Teacher still rattling off French from textbook. Most students listening attentively. Traditional seating. Students scattered all over room.	Students quite passive but listening carefully to teacher. Responding a little better as class progresses. Seem to be loosening up a bit.
9:25	J. sitting back in his chair—legs stretched out under desk—arms folded, staring passively at teacher but paying attention. Fidgety, changes position often —feet tapping on floor.	Teacher asks questions— kids laugh. First sign of humor seems to loosen kids and teacher up a bit.	Kids much more involved now. Teacher soliciting responses. Students very well behaved. More involved in lesson now. Teacher rattling off French.

50

Time	Specific behavior at 5-7 minute intervals	Environment	Impression-Comments
Period 2 **Shop**			
9:35	J. puts his safety glasses on— plugs in electric sander and begins sanding his wood project. Relaxed and joking with classmate as he sands. He's in woodshop.	Woodshop kids well motivated and anxious to get to work. Teacher reminds kids of safety rules. All kids working on projects.	Small class. Kids excited and motivated to have opportunity for hands-on experience.
9:48	J. shuts off sander and goes to friend to give him advice on his project. Returns to sanding his project. Checking out other kid's projects as he sits and sands.	Teacher very involved helping individual students. Kids talking—socializing but working on their projects.	J. is quite good with his hands. Knows exactly what he is doing—what tools he needs. Would probably be a good craftsman.
9:55	J. now hand sanding his project. Working independently and seems to know what he is doing. Looks for a tool that someone else is using. Goes to tool cabinet to get another tool. Converses briefly with a friend.	Excellent—cheery shop. Well lit—roomy. Kids relaxed and happy to be working with their hands. Absolutely no discipline problems.	Teacher claims this is his best class. Low enrollment (11 students). He's relaxed —students relaxed. All are working with exception of a girl waiting for a tool. Kids helping each other.
10:05	J. whistling happily—still hand sanding his shelf.	Still casual—friendly, hard working. Kids and teacher smiling and working cooperatively.	A few chronically disruptive students are working hard and responsibly. Love hands-on activities.
Period 3 **Math**			
10:25	Working on math homework. Sitting passively writing notes teacher is placing on board. J. rocking back and forth in his chair.	Quiet-peaceful-small class. Teacher lecture. Traditional classroom and seating. Students attentive.	Teacher-dominated. Students sitting passively and attentively.
10:40	J. still sitting attentively with legs tucked under chair. Leans over to talk to neighbor—leans back in chair, arms folded. Biting on pencil.	Teacher still dominating discussion. Continuing lecture in math. Students quiet and attentive.	Some students seem to be getting lost. Those kids are getting jittery and nervous. Kids stretching and giggling frequently.
11:05	J. talking with neighbor. Taking notes as teacher continues to lecture on math. Stretches—sits back in seat, legs under desk stretched out. Mumbles an answer that teacher asks. Looks at neighbor and laughs.	Teacher getting a little impatient with students not following him. "Stay with me," he admonishes. Kids perk up again momentarily.	Kids seemed bored, but most are trying to be attentive. Advanced math class. Very few questions. Teacher lecturing rapidly and without a break. Asks questions but he answers his own questions. Doesn't give kids a chance to answer.

51

Time	Specific behavior at 5-7 minute intervals	Environment	Impression-Comments
Period 4 *English*			
11:10	J. a lot more animated—talking —trying to converse with teacher. Interrupts another student. Knows now that I'm following him. Tells other kids, "See I told you."	Kids relaxed, talkative. Classroom bright and sunny. Classroom decorated and displayed with student work. Good student-teacher rapport evident.	This is an excellent teacher. Nominated for state teacher of year awhile back. Very dynamic, kids respond in kind.
11:20	J. taking dictation-test taped by teacher. Must write down sentences being dictated by teacher and punctuate sentences. He is fast writer and seems impatient with slowness of tape. Cracking knuckles as he waits for next sentence on tape.	Quiet and attentive as kids write diligently from tape. Now taking test. Quiet and serious atmosphere.	Again I notice a certain passivity and boredom. Only time I saw enthusiasm and motivation was during shop class. Kids doing the work but reluctantly and dolefully.
11:30	J. has pen in mouth—still taking dictation test. A little fidgety. Legs bouncing under desk. Chewing on pen as he waits impatiently for next sentence on tape.	Still quiet—serene as tape tends to lull everyone into somewhat of a stupor, including observer. I almost fall asleep. Voice on tape has hypnotic/sedative effect on me.	Teachers voice on tape is mellow and smooth. So nice that it tends to lull you off to sleep. Kids and observer begin to yawn— seems contagious.
11:40	J. still sitting quietly—now working on punctuation from dictated passage. Seems confident, not as fidgety.	Quiet—test-taking atmosphere. Everyone is working hard on test.	I notice just how hard it is for a kid to get through a day of sitting in classrooms with no opportunity to expend energy. No wonder they go bananas at lunchtime.
11:50	J. finishes early. Hands paper in. Gets up to help collate papers. Laughing and talking quietly with a girl and boy working on collating. Sits back down when teacher begins to bring class to end. Listens to teacher explain homework assignment.	Kids beginning to finish test. "Five minutes left folks," says teacher. Kids still working get a little more anxious. They are writing faster and checking the clock.	I am more and more amazed and aware of physical restrictive environment for young adolescent. Pent-up energy—no opportunity to release so far.
Lunch Time			
12:05	J. sitting with large group of friends—mostly academically oriented. Eating lunch and copying homework assignment from another student. Laughing, enjoying himself.	Lunchroom atmosphere. Kids blowing off some steam. Loud. Hungry—eating ravenously.	They certainly need this break. Seems too long a period of time for kids to sit and listen without some physical break time.
12:10	J. playing basketball with some friends. At last able to expend some energy.	Kids ecstatic to be free and outdoors for 45 minutes. Lots of activity. Running, jumping, and energy exertion.	

52

Time	Specific behavior at 5-7 minute intervals	Environment	Impression-Comments
Biology Lab			
12:50	J. is examining a vial with Drosophila (bugs). Seems to enjoy hands-on, observation kinds of activities. Smiling, seems to have perked up after lunch.	Casual—free flowing—teacher sitting among kids as they observe fruit flies in the vial.	Kids seem to be more interested and involved than in regular classroom. More enthusiasm—more activity. Seem very interested. Lots of questions and involvement.
1:00	J. gets up with other kids to continue working on lab to grow their own fruit flies. He seems the most happy and enthusiastic. He's really involved in what he's doing. Again, hands-on experiences bring out the best in him.	Trusting lab situation. Kids are mature and responsible. Teacher is basically functioning as a facilitator. Kids working independently and effectively.	Amazed at what kids can do when given the responsibility and opportunity. They're *all* interested and involved and working. Allowed freedom of movement. Not restricted to seats.
1:15	J. still working assiduously on his lab project with other students. His enthusiasm is sustained. He seems happier and more alive with this hands-on experience. Similar to his shop experience.	Very casual, but time on task is maximized as kids work hard to complete this phase of lab.	Can't believe how much more motivated and turned on kids are with hands-on activities.
1:30	J. still working hard on lab even though lab time is up. Doesn't want to clean up—would prefer to keep working.	Kids clean up. Very responsible lab aide knows exactly what to do. Good training by teacher to assume responsibility.	
Regular Biology Class			
1:40	J. takes a quiz. Seems confident as he takes it. Seems much looser than he was at beginning of day. Gets up and walks around when the test is over. Kids around with his neighbor.	Regular classroom situation. Students are seated as teacher reviews answers with students. Kids are talkative but it is relevant to classwork.	Kids are back to sitting, listening, and responding intermittently. While kids are reading answers about half of class turned off or distracted.
2:00	J. is called on to answer one of the questions. Answer is perfect. He smiles when he is congratulated by teacher. Laughs with neighbor after commendation.	Traditional science classroom situation. Teacher leads discussion and review. Asks many questions. Challenges deductive and inductive reasoning skills of his students.	Good climate for thinking students. Teacher encourages inquiry learning.
2:10	J. seems much more interested and alive. Getting a little tired—yawning often but smiling. More and more relaxed. Fidgeting a lot in seat. Answering many of the questions.	Filmstrip being shown on heredity and characteristics. Students are responsive and relatively enthusiastic.	Teacher keeps students alert by his constant inquiry type questioning.

53

Time	Specific behavior at 5-7 minute intervals	Environment	Impression-Comments
2:20	J. getting very fidgety—rocking back and forth. Still listening but getting more distant look on face. Appears full of nervous energy.	Filmstrip still being shown —kids beginning to get tired now that end of day is nearing. Lots of yawning.	Kids are tired as well as *observer*. It's a long day for adolescent students. One more class—thank God!

Social Studies

2:30	J. sitting in library talking to four other students. Working on research papers for social studies. Lots of joking and frivolous behavior. Legs moving rapidly—seems anxious and anticipating end of day.	Library situation. Kids doing research. Lots of interaction with librarian and social studies teacher. Kids seem motivated but tired, lots of movement.	End of day coming. Kids seem to be anticipating this —are excitable. Observer is also anticipating end of day. It's been a long, long day.

End-of-Day Interview

1. What do you like best about this school?

   A lot of things, mainly my friends. The teachers are nice and I like soccer after school. I like almost everything about the school.

2. What one thing would you change about the school if you could?

   I like the way it is except for the extreme temperature changes in the corridors.

3. What is the best thing that happened to you in school today? This year?

   When I found out I wasn't being tailed.

   The soccer team was a lot of fun. I made some good goals.

4. What is the worst thing that happened to you in school today?

   When I found out I was being tailed.

   The worst thing that happened was when I tore the cartilage in my knee.

5. How would you describe this school to a newcomer?

   It's nice and a good school. Watch out for some of the kids. If you do anything bad, you will get caught.

6. If you had a personal problem and wanted assistance is there someone here at school that you would readily turn to for advice?
   Friends or the guidance counselor.

Observer's Reactions

My first reaction was that this was an education for me, and I highly recommend it to other school officials. Two things stand out as I review the day:

1. It's a long day for the adolescent student, and a restrictive one. There is a lot of sitting and listening with minimal opportunity for expending energy that most adolescents have a lot of.

2. For the most part, the ninth grade student is most receptive to hands-on activities. Enthusiasm and interest seem to peak when he or she is allowed to participate actively in classroom experiences. Interest and enthusiasm seem lowest when student is required to sit still and listen for any extended period of time.

I was very impressed with the quality of instruction that I observed throughout the school day. Teachers maximized time on task and all were working hard to complete the day's objectives. Most teachers were veterans and paid little attention to my presence as they went about their business of teaching and facilitating learning.

What I did learn is that the students' and teachers' day is an exhausting one; mentally for the student and mentally and physically for the teacher.

I am more convinced than ever that hands-on experiences and activities produce the most enthusiastic responses from the adolescent. Extended periods of time without diversified experiences diminish attention span, interest, and motivation. Diversifying instructional strategies at frequent intervals significantly helps to sustain and maintain attention and interest.

I would like to see a more thematic and interdisciplinary approach to learning. Following a student schedule for a day offered me the opportunity to experience what the student experiences. There is a lot of fragmentation. Interdisciplinary relevancy is minimal, if not nonexistent. A student hops from probability, to China, to sentence mechanics, to heredity, in a three-hour span of time with approach to and content entirely different with barely a thread of relevancy existing.

This is not a condemnation, but rather an observation of a situation. Is it possible to create an effective interdisciplinary approach to learning without sacrificing basic skills along the way? Perhaps similar approaches and methods in different disciplines might help to bring knowledge together.

In summation, the experience was an enlightening and positive one for me as the observer. I can now be more sensitive to the needs of the transescent. The school day should be planned to reflect the physical and emotional needs of the adolescent, with more opportunity to expend energy, more opportunities for hands-on experiences and activities, and more attention to factors that are common to different bodies of knowledge to give more relevancy to the learning process.

Shadow Study Number 6

Conducted in a small-town comprehensive six-year high school with 150 pupils enrolled. The student was 15 years old and was classified as above average.

Time	Specific behavior at 5-7 minute intervals	Environment	Impressions-Comments
8:30	S. in chair, second row, paying attention to CPR lecture being given by volunteer instructors from the community. Responding to questions asked of the class by the instructors from time to time as requested. S. is not as actively involved in discussion questions as some of the other students.	Practice gym with chairs arranged in two rows for CPR lecture by community volunteers from the EMR unit. Steel gym building with carpeted floor; metal folding chairs in two rows for students.	Entire class paying close attention.
8:35	Lecture continues—still paying close attention.	Facilities available in gymnasium are not conducive to a lecture situation.	

Time	Specific behavior at 5-7 minute intervals	Environment	Impression-Comments
8:40	Sitting quietly, listening, some movement as S. tries to arrange himself comfortably in metal folding chair—appears to be getting uncomfortable.		
8:45	Up to get copy of test and answer sheet. Uses chair for a "desk" and sits on floor to take test.	Facilities in gymnasium not very conducive to a testing situation.	Good attention and participation by overall class during the CPR section of the PE course makes a class atmosphere that somewhat offsets the physical limitations of the gym for lectures and testing.
8:50	Has moved around a bit, adjusting for discomfort, but working on written test. Some interruptions as students ask questions and receive oral answers from instructors. S. raises hand and also asks a question regarding some section of the CPR test.		
8:55	Working quietly on test.	For several minutes, almost no noise or distraction—all class is working on test. Occasional questions being answered by instructors on a one-to-one basis.	
9:00	Working quietly on test.		
9:05	Talking quietly to one instructor after asking a question.		
9:10	Working quietly on test.		
9:15	Has completed and handed in test, has moved to another area of gym to observe CPR demonstration.	Class concludes, puts up chairs, and leaves the room.	
9:20	In chair with music folder. Talking quietly before first song.	Vocal music room. Tiered rows of chairs, piano/directors' stand on lowest level in front of the classroom. Seating arranged by vocal sections (soprano, alto, etc.) with boys on the back two rows.	S. obviously enjoys this class. Actively involved with the singing.
9:25	Sitting quietly while another group's section is being rehearsed.		
9:30	Singing.		
9:35	Singing.		

Time	Specific behavior at 5-7 minute intervals	Environment	Impression-Comments
9:45	Between songs. Talking with other students while director and accompanist are discussing next song.	Class setting is informal yet highly productive for vocal music. Students have "breaks" after each two to three songs to talk, get a drink, etc. Class situation is very conducive to good rehearsals and practice.	
9:50	Singing.		
9:55	Sitting quietly doing homework or assignment from another class. Girls' sections are singing.		
10:00	Sitting quietly doing homework while girls are singing.		
10:05	Has put up music, is passing to third period.		
10:05	S. in class and working on art project.	Art room. Much equipment and many student work desks. The students move around in a relaxed atmosphere.	
10:11	Quietly reading an assignment from reference materials.		S. has already completed his silk screen assignment and is "waiting for the class to get ready to go on" with next assignment. Several students have not completed silk screening.
10:17	Asked instructor to go to the rest room—returns quickly and continues reading. (Was not "followed" into rest room.)	Much individualized teacher assistance. Teacher moves from student to student as needed; majority of students are proceeding without assistance.	
10:24	Discussing academic contest that he participated in on Monday with other students, who show interest in his achievements.		
10:31	Joined other class members in a discussion of yesterday's lyceum/ seminar on premarital counseling.		The entire school spent the previous day with the lyceum/seminar and the class as a whole expressed interest in the ideas that the guest presented.
10:38	Working on reading assignment.		

Time	Specific behavior at 5-7 minute intervals	Environment	Impression-Comments
10:45	Making plans for art class silver jewelry project.		Several project books for jewelry are available in the classroom. S. is reviewing them.
10:51	Working out details for jewelry project. Class dismissed for activity period.		
10:54- 11:25	Class meeting not observed as observer needed to attend observer meeting.		
11:25	Has picked up music folder and instrument. In his seat warming up for band. Joking with another student prior to beginning of band practice.	Band room. Similar set-up to vocal music room. Tiered rows for seating. S. at right end of second row with saxophone section.	Obviously another class that S. enjoys. Described by teacher as "never disruptive and musically gifted."
11:30	Warming up with saxophone for class practice.		Becoming *very* aware that "someone is watching him."
11:35	Listening to band director as a discussion is presented for first number.	The band/vocal music director is one of the most student-oriented instructors in the school. An informal/relaxed atmosphere prevails for all students. A great deal of praise is given to students (individually and as a group) by the instructor.	
11:40	Playing saxophone with band.		
11:45	Playing saxophone with band.		
11:50	Talking quietly to another member of saxophone section while brass sections work on a portion of the piece being practiced.		
11:55	Playing saxophone with band.		
12:00	Sitting quietly while director discusses a portion of the practice with the class.		
12:05	Playing saxophone with band.		
12:10	Talking with other students during "break" between numbers.		

Time	Specific behavior at 5-7 minute intervals	Environment	Impression-Comments
12:15	Putting up instrument and music folder; preparing to leave class for lunch. Much talking among all students; S. actively involved.		
12:20	Has left classroom for lunch.	Students on "open campus" during lunch period.	
1:00	Class has been in session for five minutes. S. is working on an assignment for another class while the instructor is lecturing.	Math class (Algebra I). The instructor is lecturing. The mathematics classroom is in an "out-of-the-way" area on the second floor of the high school, in the "quietest" section of the building.	
1:14	The student is working on the other assignment.	One student is enrolled in "independent study" in computer math; the remainder of the class is enrolled in Algebra I. The instructor is lecturing to the students.	
1:21	Talking to another student briefly, and returning to work on the other assignment.	The lecture portion of the period completed, the instructor is answering individual student questions.	
1:28	The student is working on the other assignment.		
1:35	Talking to another student briefly, returning to work on the other assignment.		
1:40	General talking throughout the classroom. The student is talking quietly as he waits for the dismissal bell.		The class will end in one minute.
1:45	S. entered classroom, sat down, and began typing.	Typing class. Straight rows of typewriter tables with electric typewriters. Substitute teacher.	
1:50	Received permission and left room for drink of water. Returned and resumed typing.		
1:55	Setting margins on typewriter. Resumed typing.		
2:00	Has quit typing and is reading a magazine article.		Supposed to be typing.

59

Time	Specific behavior at 5-7 minute intervals	Environment	Impression-Comments
2:05	Talking to another student.	Informed by substitute that he is supposed to be typing, but that he doesn't have to. Is also informed that regardless, the assignment is due "tomorrow."	
2:10	The student is typing again.		The observer is trying very hard not to laugh.
2:17	Student is typing, frustrated, mumbling "Well . . . well . . . well . . ." to himself.		
2:24	The student is typing.		The observer has regained control.
2:30	Signing name to homework and turning it in.	English class. Traditional seating in rows. S. sits in first seat, first row, at far left side of classroom.	
2:35 to 2:50	Entire class, including S., is taking a test. S. working quietly on the test.		
2:55	Working on class assignment that is due.	Classroom is 1931 vintage, like most of the academic building classrooms. High windows, plaster walls, painted. Wall-to-wall posters "decorate" the classroom.	The class assignment that is due is the same assignment that the student was working on in math and typing.
3:00	Trading papers and preparing to grade. Talking with neighboring student.		
3:05	Grading papers with the class.	According to instructor, S. is a "happy" student, ready to work, concerned that he's not doing enough— right enough. He tries to "please."	
3:10	Figuring grades. In turn, reports grade of the paper that he has graded.		
3:15	Working on tomorrow's homework assignment.		
3:20	I leave the room for the end-of-day interview. Instructor has S. come to the office for the end-of-day interview as soon as I leave.		This was an overall busy day for S. I admit that I am glad that he found enough time to get his English homework done.

End-of-Day Interview

1. What do you like best about this school?

   The size of the school, and you get more individual help from the teachers.

   Q - Just help, or do you mean that your teachers know you better than if you were in a larger school?

   A - That too.

2. What one thing would you change about the school if you could?

   The *appearance!*

   Note: The school was built in 1931. The outside appearance is still nice; however, the classrooms and interior of the school are deteriorating. Students are very much aware that two recent bond issues have failed miserably at the polls. Many of the students feel that the community does not provide much support for the school, the school district, or the students.

3. What is the best thing that happened to you in school today? This year?

   I got all of my assignments done . . . finally.

   (Year) The band trips and state fair.

4. What is the worst thing that happened to you in school today? This year?

   Getting a B in English.

5. How would you describe this school to a newcomer?

   I think that it is easy to make good friends and we get more privileges here than in most schools.

6. If you had a personal problem and wanted assistance is there someone here at school that you would readily turn to for advice?

   The high school guidance counselor.

Observer's Reactions

Having spent a day observing a ninth grade student, some of my reactions, feelings, and judgments are:

The student was selected by pulling a student file at random. The student selected is not necessarily "typical" of the students in the ninth grade of this high school; he is an extremely good student with a high GPA and a high degree of achievement in several areas. He is, for example, described by his band/vocal music instructor as "musically gifted."

One of my first reactions was that I wondered if the writers of *Nation at Risk* had been involved in such a study in the setting of a small, agriculturally oriented high school in a small town. I doubt this, because if the members of the group had included such visitations in their study, I can only assume that some of their conclusions would not have been quite so strong.

Even as a building principal, having spent considerable evaluation time in each teacher's classroom during the past eight school years, I was again amazed at the variety and intensity of the individual student's school day.

The students are busier than many of us would like to believe. The amount of time consumed by school classwork and school activities is staggering. Few adults would consider putting in as much time on their jobs as the majority of ninth grade students put into their schooling.

Although the study "follows" only one student, the observer cannot avoid viewing the overall group throughout the day. I was, perhaps, not the most impartial observer, and my capacity as building principal in a school small enough that I am known by each student in all probability made some differences in classroom behavior throughout the day. Even with this in mind, I could not help but to be very much impressed with the activities of *all* students—not only with the activities and load of the student being observed specifically.

My final conclusion after participating in this study is that the study helped me by providing a very refreshing insight into an "overall school day" in "my" school. The overview of a "typical school day" made me feel that there is a great deal of learning going on and that the American high school may not be in as horrible a shape as some critics would have the public believe.

Postscript

As an addendum to this chapter, 15 of the individual observer's reactions are included. They are not necessarily representative, although they well may be; they were selected because it was believed readers would appreciate some of the perceptiveness of the observers and some of the interesting analyses they provided.

The bell rang and class periods began, and the bell rang and the class periods ended. Students moved from classroom to classroom in an orderly manner. There were no discipline problems. The teachers were considerate and helpful to students and cordial to each other.

But something was missing. I wanted and, indeed, expected to see evidence of enthusiasm. There was very little. I wanted to observe meaningful interaction between teachers and students and among teachers and students. There was very little. I wanted to observe instances of critical thinking. There were very few.

Instruction was based almost entirely on textbooks, and the lessons were little more than academic exercises, complete with chalkboard and seatwork. Correct answers appeared to be the major concern, while there was little or no evidence of creative thinking.

What a day! A real education for me. Overall, I am very impressed with the school—facilities, teachers, administration, and kids. As a middle-school teacher I marveled at the "new" maturity exhibited by ninth graders (some of whom I taught as seventh graders).

I was impressed that for the main part every minute was utilized constructively. I saw very little time wasted, very few discipline problems, lots of instruction. Not one teacher sat down at his or her desk the entire day.

The curriculum offered this student a real variety of classwork—the day went by fast. Teachers treated students with respect and vice-versa—all here seemed to be proud of their school.

One teacher noted that there were few discipline problems because there was no time for them—students and teachers alike knew there were better things to do, and everyone had his or her own responsibilities to carry out. Shannon said that ninth graders had to act mature or they wouldn't "fit in" with upper classmen.

The most startling thing is the amount of frontal teaching that goes on. Teacher domination of the classroom is incredibly high. To me there were great opportunities to involve the students in learning and have them actively pursue knowledge, yet it was not happening. The students seen today were essentially passive recipients of factual knowledge.

My student enjoyed band and physical education because he was actively involved all period long in both classes. Granted this was physical activity, but one does not have to manipulate or be physically involved to be engaged in active education. I think that teachers, even the good ones, have simply found it easier, for whatever reason, to deliver their lessons in the ways observed today. I asked my student if he would consider this a typical day and he said, "Yes sir, for the most part."

I was overwhelmed by the sameness of each class, the sitting and listening, the general passive role of the student and a general mild blah feeling at the end of the day. I wasn't bored by any means, yet I feel kind of sorry for the students, especially since I shadowed a well-adjusted young person of above average intelligence, generally involved in the total school program. What is it like for a child of average or lower ability who is not involved in the school community?

If I had not seen this student's class schedule (had not seen that she was in both an advanced math and English class) and had not had an interview with her, I would have assumed from observation that she was not much of a student. Her behavior in class gave the impression of indifference. Her responses were timid, if at all.

She did mention in the interview that she thought school started too early, and she did fall asleep during the movie so possibly she was extremely tired today, and that tiredness came across as indifference. It would appear she has a group of friends she is comfortable with, as she was not very friendly in general in her classes.

I saw little expression on her face and little response to student or teacher remarks. She was much more animated during the interview. She does not feel that her academic load is difficult and that adjustment to high school was difficult. She does like the freedom of high school.

My day of shadowing a ninth grade student in our 7-12 high school was not only an informative experience for me, but a real "eye opener."

The student I observed for the day is enrolled in a general curriculum, taking math, English, science, art, physical education, and French classes. She is a most active person and never stopped moving from the time I first started the day with her til 3 p.m. when we closed the day with the interview. She said she was not aware that I was shadowing her all day.

I was surprised at how easy our teachers apparently are on the students. The student I shadowed only had homework in two classes, and was given extra class time to work on this homework. The physical education class offered no instruction today whatsoever. The students were simply required to dress, play, shower, and they could pass the class. Only two of the classes today even used their textbooks, also.

The student I followed had a nice variety of classes. Her first hour required active student participation. The next class was a quiet individual work-at-desk activity. Third hour, the teacher lectured, asked for some student participation, and then gave the students time to write in class. Our school only allows a half hour lunch break, which has proved to be an appropriate amount of time.

The afternoon classes provided, first, very active participation for physical education. A quiet period came next when the student watched a movie, and then worked individually on an art project, then back to a lecture class where students question and have a chance to have guided practice in class. This variety, plus the five-minute breaks between classes and the half-hour lunch break in the middle of the day made this student's schedule an interesting educational experience.

As indicated on the hourly observation sheets, this student appeared interested in her classes and was also on task for the majority of the classroom time.

Our school offers different levels of science and math to the freshman students, and the classes I was in yesterday were the lower level areas. The composition of the class appeared to be well served at this level.

Enjoyable, but very tiring day.

The day in the life of an academic ninth grader is rush, rush, rush. A student has a complete schedule, with no breaks from academics until lunch time. The movement from class to class in a time limit of three minutes does not give you a moment to say hi to a friend without being tardy.

A student reacts almost involuntarily as suddenly out of nowhere she leans, turns, and makes a comment to a fellow student.

Laura reacted to a stressful situation in a health class, where a movie was shown on an alcoholic mother. Her behavior changed in that she became a part of the scene, wringing her hands and becoming tense.

I was shadowing an above average academic student who enjoyed school and was full of vigor and vitality. Some of her peers were not quite as alert or as attentive.

The day is long for a ninth grader, and full of academic pressures. The passing of classes and use of restroom facilities cannot be done in the allotted time. I was thoroughly exhausted and I did not have the responsibility of retaining any academic information from all the instructors. Most instructors during my visit lectured or taught for the full 42 minutes. Some classes got to be a drag for me as they were teacher-oriented only.

I enjoyed the experience and feel that to follow an average student, who is nonacademic, I would find more difficulties and dislike for school.

The environment at S. encourages independence. There is no homeroom period; students go directly to their first period class. Although there are no bells to indicate period changes, students were in their seats ready to work at the appropriate time. Many were comfortable and free in their dialog with teachers; some were not. The ninth graders seem fairly mature and physically suited for the high school.

C. appears to be an average or below average student, more concerned about socialization than academics. Although grades are a concern to her, she does not seem to have the self-discipline or the motivation to work hard. Her teachers appear to accept this and make little or no effort to draw her out or to help her better understand the material.

The brighter, more motivated students sit toward the front of the classroom and carry the conversation. Those who are not interested comfortably sit to the rear and do not participate. As long as they're not disruptive, they're left alone.

C. and the few others who did not actively participate in the math class would have learned more if they had worked with this fine teacher, in a smaller class, at a slower pace. These students were missing a great deal of material and were probably embarrassed to join in the discussion because the other students were grasping the information so quickly.

The less motivated students appear to need greater external controls in order to focus on their work: more direct supervision, closer observation, explicit and higher expectations, more encouragement and support from adults.

C. is shy and sensitive to criticism. Her responses during the interview kept focusing on her teachers. She mentioned that she would ask her friends for help with work but would not want to go to her teachers. Some of them made her feel "stupid" and inadequate. She is not having success in learning, but she is getting something positive from her peers. There is a great need for her to feel good about herself. C. expressed the desire to have a dean or someone "know her better." The student's need for continuing adult support on a more intimate level is an aspect of education that needs attention. Brief and fragmented contact with teachers does not meet this need.

Time was not used effectively or efficiently in many of the classes. Improved teaching methods and more active student participation would help combat boredom in the classroom. Teachers who enjoy what they do generate more interest than those who don't.

The following questions came to mind by the end of the day:

- Do students have to be failing to receive tutorial help? Peer tutoring is available in this school. Why hasn't this been communicated to C., and why doesn't someone encourage her to take advantage of it before she is failing?
- Is it already accepted that C. is just an average student and will not be expected to do any better?
- Must students become discipline problems in order to receive attention from guidance counselors or deans?
- Why do teachers proceed with new material when it's obvious that many of the students aren't fully understanding that which has already been covered? (French was a prime example.)
- Should the curriculum be revised to permit teachers more time to cover less material more thoroughly?
- Isn't the process of learning more important than the amount covered?
- Why are teachers giving average students the impression that they are inadequate if they don't understand the teacher's explanation the first, second, or third time? Can it be due in part to the teacher's frustration resulting from insufficient knowledge of alternate teaching methods?
- How can school personnel become more sensitive to the issue of self-esteem?

Reactions

The ninth grade has a very interesting schedule. There is so much activity going on in class, between classes, and at lunch that I was very tired at the end of the day.

The student I shadowed had a most unusual schedule, in that I walked around the school in almost a complete circle following him. I realize that his schedule made sense and that this "touring" only happens when the periods are in the order they were in today.

Feelings

Jealousy!! I would love to be a ninth grade student here at the junior high.

Sympathy!! Sam is grouped with some students who think school is a joke.

Empathy!! I can relate to Sam's ability in math and science and his shortcomings in social studies and English. Mine are the opposite.

Joy!! The ninth grade seems to be fun for all of the ninth graders.

Judgments

My personal judgment is that we, as secondary teachers, could do a lot more for the "middle" student of average intelligence. Sam had much more to offer than the time or class size would allow.

Sam was also in a group with students that wanted to be "stars" no matter what behavior they must display. Sam plodded on, doing his work.

After following Sam's schedule all day, I now know more about why my afternoon classes are so difficult to settle down.

I am currently principal of the Middle School, grades 5-8, in our school district. I have previous experience as principal in a senior high and seven years as a 7-12 grade principal. I initiated this study assuming that the senior high was the appropriate placement for the ninth grade.

I believe the student that I shadowed today is not a typical ninth grader in our school system. I have been informed by teachers and the principal in the senior high that she is one of the few ninth graders who has taken up strong relationships with members of the senior class, both boys and girls.

In our school district I believe the ninth grade is placed with the senior high for several reasons. One of the most important reasons is that the most appropriate facilities for meeting the needs of the ninth graders, including expanded media facilities as well as vocational and science facilities are at the senior high. It also gives them an opportunity to participate in extracurricular activities at the senior high level. I believe that they have more in common with the senior high students than they do with junior high age students.

Classes that I observed were structured, yet allowed a degree of individual freedom and tolerance for the students to move around and talk and exhibit other behaviors typical of adolescence.

I also believe closing the noon hour and prohibiting students from driving during the school day would help make the senior high a better place for ninth grade students to be. I believe that currently some of them are exposed to drugs and/or other kinds of activities which may be undesirable as ninth graders, simply because they can ride with older students in their vehicles during noon hour. Since this can be done during the school day it may be done without the parents' knowledge.

I don't know if today was a typical day as far as student work and homework; however, I believe that the students could handle an increased amount of homework and more direct time-on-task activities in some of the academic classes.

Ninth grade students that I observed appeared to be happy in school, and enjoyed their day. I observed no students that I thought were too immature to be in the senior high setting.

I took the middle initial of one of the counselors ("D"), then checked the alphabetical roster, and discovered I had 11 names on the list. I then asked the secretary to give me a number between 0 and 11. She stated 5. The girl I observed was fifth on the list.

I couldn't have been more delighted than to "shadow" this particular student during the day. She is certainly above average, a student who is held in high regard by her peers, one whom I discovered is serious about her education, and one who, for the most part, was on task throughout my observation period.

She is from a divorced home, but her mother is a nurse and I sense has reinforced successfully the need for an education. I was really impressed with the manner Anne stayed on task during the day. She did not socialize to the extent many of her contemporaries, but she was not aloof or anti-social either.

She gave me the impression of being well organized (her books, notebooks, etc.). Even though I tried to make myself inconspicuous in the classroom she did not give any indication during these times that she might have been the target of the visit. She did admit to me during our conference that she began to wonder about the third period why I was in her language arts class too, when she had noticed me in algebra, general business, and advisory. But, she is the kind of student who probably would have never asked what I was doing.

She was pleased that she could be part of the research project. I got the impression that even though she enjoyed her former school, she really appreciated the opportunities provided in our building. I know this is a judgment call on my part but her responses to the questions would support this notion.

Although I didn't know the girl real well, I remember visiting with her and the mother when they enrolled. That was some time ago. The impressions I got from the teachers later were that she certainly was a good student to watch—that she is really a nice girl, and there are never any concerns regarding classroom management. I believe she is rather popular and has many friends. She certainly was a mature young lady.

Because of these conclusions, I almost feel guilty that she was the kind of student to be observed. What I have shared with you may not be a typical summary of ninth graders in our building. What I observed other students doing in the classes I visited may be more significant in this study.

I'm referring to lack of motivation, disinterest, idleness at times, extreme levels of socializing, not on task, etc. But this was not the case with Anne's performance. I would have been pleased to claim that all of our ninth graders performed in the manner demonstrated by Anne, but we all know that is not the case.

I found the day to be very tedious and I felt that the life of a ninth grader was not an easy one. I was amazed at the remarkable control and restraint exhibited by the children in a school that hardly allows breathing room because it is so overcrowded.

My subject was a fine young man who was very serious about his studies and is especially interested in the areas of math and science. He would be a credit to any student body.

The faculty and administration of the school were especially courteous and helpful to me. The school was warm, friendly, and accommodating.

Obviously P.S. feels the same warmth and concern, because in his interview with me he was very positive in his feelings about the school.

I was able to view the school day from the viewpoint of a quiet and well-behaved ninth grade girl.

One of the most obvious observations to be made was her atypical "passing period" behavior. During this five-minute break between classes, the hallways were quite boisterous with talking, laughing, and yelling; a lot of playful physical contact was made between students. K. in no way involved herself in any of this outgoing group behavior. She consistently went to her locker alone, got her materials, and walked either alone or with one friend to her next class.

Her classroom conduct also demonstrated individual rather than conformist behavior. In most instances, K. quietly and efficiently involved herself in the class assignment and refrained from talking or interacting with others. She did not appear to be particularly motivated to do more than was required, however.

I observed a break in this consistent behavior pattern in two classes, the first being physical education.

During this period, K. was much more relaxed and outgoing. This was one of the few times when I saw her talking, laughing, and joking with others. She enthusiastically participated in the activity.

The other behavior change occurred in science class, where the seating changed from a single desk row arrangement to a double person table situation.

At this point K. had someone directly next to her to speak to, and since that class was not particularly under control, her behavior reflected the looseness of structure. She did contain her talking to her neighbor, however, while other students felt the need to repeatedly vocalize opinions out loud.

The one other time K.'s behavior seemed to be uncharacteristic of the outwardly expressive ninth graders and general student body was during lunch. Semi-loud rock music was played in the cafeteria while the kids ate, thus creating a relaxed, tension-free environment. The majority of students ate and interacted with several different groups of people, while K. remained low-key and isolated herself with two other girls. She did not display the same high level of energy seen in most others.

Although K.'s actions were primarily solitary and unassuming, I did not sense any negative or anti-social attitudes evidenced by that behavior. Other students seemed to respect the way she was and did not inflict their opinions or actions upon her.

Overall, I felt that K. was a separate entity from the mainstream of the ninth grade class as well as the rest of the student population. She never engaged in any of the classroom, hallway, or lunchroom antics and maintained a quiet, reserved demeanor throughout a busy school day.

I thoroughly enjoyed the day. After three years away from ninth graders, it was a pleasure to be with ninth graders for the day and see how they learn. In many ways, they are like middle school students. In other ways they are really like senior high students.

My fear was that I would see seven lectures by seven different teachers during the course of the day. This was obviously not the case. I saw effective middle level teachers working with ninth grade students at the proper level. The program was clearly geared to the maturity level of the students.

But, there were many techniques and approaches that were similar to techniques and approaches in the middle school. There were hands-on activities, there was a variety of activities, teachers using overhead projectors, students went to the board to do problems, and the pacing was good. With these similarities, however, there were clearly some differences.

The attention span of ninth grade students is unmistakably longer than that of seventh or eighth graders. They could and did remain on task for longer periods of time. It was also evident that the teachers had conditioned them to learn certain routines and procedures. With just a simple cue word, pupils followed these routines individually, consistently, and in a way that reflected their maturity. Seventh and eighth grade students would have needed reinforcement; the ninth graders could do it all by themselves.

I was also impressed with the creativity of many of the teachers. In a number of cases, pupils were actively involved in creative activities. I was a bit concerned, however, that there were a couple of periods where the youngsters were entirely too passive. I believe that the youngsters learn more when they are more actively involved. I think this is as true of ninth graders as it is of sixth, seventh, and eighth graders.

In conclusion, I felt the learning needs of the ninth grade students that I observed in general yesterday and the one student whom I shadowed in particular were being met. These were teachers trained in middle level education who ran a good school and showed that they cared about kids.

If the ninth grade student fares as well in the 9 to 12 senior high and the junior/senior high, I will feel very comfortable with the 6, 7, 8 organization. On the other hand, if the reports of ninth graders in senior high schools describe more passive activities or a more passive day, perhaps we need to look more carefully at how the high school is trying to meet the needs of the ninth grade student.

The day is truly a long one with few moments for socialization with peers. Other than a brief period for lunch, a ninth grade student is continually moving. It was a pleasure to see good solid teaching occurring. Little time is wasted within the class period. It was unfortunate to observe that a student with poor listening skills is at a definite disadvantage. Most of the activity occurring is by the teacher and the student is a listener.

Homework was assigned in every class and was reviewed. Some assignments were collected, while others were not. The student observed would be classified as an average student. His total vocalization during the entire day, with the exception of the lunch period, amounted to one paragraph. It is easy to see how students such as these get "lost" and are unrecognized by their classroom teachers.

Classroom behavior was excellent. Standards have been established, are known by the students, and are adhered to. It was distressing to observe that in all of the class preparations little carry-over occurred from the previous day's lesson. The period just began. None of the lessons were summarized—just ended.

At the end of the day I was tired. For a large number of students, the day continues after other students have gone. Extracurricular activities now begin. When arriving home at 6:00 p.m., homework must then be started. Few adults could keep the pace up for any prolonged period of time.

The experience for me was well worth the time and effort. Every staff member should be afforded this same opportunity to see what school is really like.

My initial reactions were as follows:

I was glad to see that this ninth grader had some fine teachers. It looked to me as if learning was going on and students were really being taught. I gained new perceptions of the teachers. I was interested that the room arrangements of two of the first three classes (Spanish and computers) were radically different from the usual rows with the teacher up front.

Also the health class was held in a biology lab with lab stations jutting out into the room. Chair desks were in the central area of the room and gave the class a large appearance. There was definitely variety in room arrangement, teacher approach, and the nature of activities in which the student had the opportunity to participate.

Another reaction that I have is that student teachers and even more experienced teachers may need more help in confronting stressful situations.

Most of all, however, I was struck by the fact that I did not see George smile until after lunch in the geometry class, when he actually entered into some exchange with other students. I wondered how many others there were who went through the days like that. School appeared to be a rather lonely time. I felt he needed more reinforcement during the context of the day.

George is a good student, a self-motivated one, but he does not stand out in a crowd. I looked for him at lunch; he told me he saw me but I missed him. He also did not assert himself very much. He did go up and ask a question of the computer and geometry teachers, but they appeared routine.

Related to the above observation is one about the personalization of education. Education did not seem very personal. No papers were received back. I did not observe anyone, 69 neither teacher nor student, speaking casually to him except in fourth period geometry class.

He had opportunities to respond (usually in the group) in the Spanish class; he was checked by the student teacher in the English class that had gone to the library; and the computer teacher also monitored his lesson, but there did not seem to be much connection.

He was doing what he was supposed to be doing. He appeared interested in reading for one project and extended the time on both ends of the period working on his own. He was quietly taking responsibility for his own learning. He was courteous. If America has a generation of kids like this, I think we will be all right.

I am sorry, however, that we did not evoke more visible enthusiasm in him during the school day. I shall be watching to see if it does occur, and then I will be wondering how this young man turns out.

_____

CHAPTER 6

Conclusions and Recommendations

T he value of the school experience for ninth graders—regardless of the specific deficiencies of any school—cannot be overlooked. School is significant in the lives of ninth graders. School is the source of many needed lessons, whether learned from teachers, peers, or self. Were it not for schools, youth would be seriously deficient in the acquisition of information, the development of social skills, the maturing of the mind, the evolving of a positive self-concept, and in many other ways.

Society is dependent on schools for many functions including, but not limited to, the acquisition of basic skills and knowledge.

Such a point of view is needed lest the analysis which follows, and which might seem to emphasize deficiencies and weaknesses, be taken out of context and the weakness be considered even more critical than they are.

Yet, at the same time, knowing the importance of education and the varied responsibilities given our schools, it behooves us to do the very best we can to provide the most effective environment possible. The times demand more of our schools than merely providing a safe custodial environment for youth.

The question, "How fares the ninth grade?" cannot be answered easily or categorically. While the answer, "not so well," would be quite fair from some standpoints, it could be viewed as a subtle indictment that failed to take into account the many excellent programs and effective teachers that do exist. On the other hand, the answer, "okay," would be fair from another standpoint, although it would be an abrogation of professional responsibility.

While a single generalization cannot and should not be offered as an answer to the major question addressed by this study, significant data and many partial answers were discovered. The findings provide some clear pictures, raise many questions, clarify some assumptions, confirm some suspicions, and establish a sound base for examining and improving ninth grade programs no matter where they exist.

Educators responsible for the education of ninth graders should ponder the results of this research project and see wherein there are clear leads for strengthening their programs.

As one tries to pull together the range of generalizations and characteristics of ninth grade programs that emerge from this study, one can find much to support a feeling of optimism. The basic ingredients for excellence are at hand. The behavior of ninth grade students is very acceptable, even excellent. No blackboard jungles appear to exist.

From the standpoint of physical facilities, schools, for the most part, are adequate and often outstanding. The learning environment of individual classrooms is usually good, as 71 teachers strive to make them attractive and subject-relevant. Sufficient books and materials are nearly always available.

Teachers are capable and conscientious, and are both liked and respected by students. Students enjoy school and speak about their schools in glowing terms. Students are busy; they are not wasting their time on insignificant electives to the detriment of basic subjects. And, a well-established administrative framework brings the elements of the schooling process together in a smoothly operating organization.

No revolution is necessary. No wholesale apple-cart upsetting is called for; no mass hiring and firing is needed. No reorganization of grades seems mandated. No longer school day or school year is indicated. No major alteration in the subjects offered is required.

On the other hand, the results of this study are disquieting. While conditions are not bad, they do leave much to be desired. Ninth graders are treated well, but the full range of their needs does not seem to be met as well as it might. Student apathy and passivity are evident, and little intellectual challenge or meaningful interaction is occurring. Classroom lessons are all too often limited to the coverage of textbook content.

But we must also be reminded that while 141 school reports may indeed lead cumulatively to valid generalization, the process is not reversible. That is, the generalizations which emerge from the large group cannot and should not be applied to any *one* of the schools that comprise that group. With that caveat, here are some things that can be said about the *group*.

Some Clearly Positive Generalizations

When compiled into a big picture, the snapshots of ninth grade education taken on March 7, 1984, yield a good many bright spots. Emerging from the reports are a number of generalizations that are both positive and encouraging. They counter many widely-held assumptions about the state of public education.

1. Schools for ninth graders, whatever the organizational pattern in which they are located, are well organized and running smoothly. Although observers were not asked to evaluate the overall organization and operational procedures, many did. Without exception, the observers who commented did so in terms of praise and admiration. Despite large numbers of students, the need to move them regularly from place to place, to feed them, and to provide for their physical as well as their educational needs, schools seemed to run almost like clockwork.

2. Physical facilities, for the most part, are quite adequate and maintenance is good. Naturally, the age and quality of the physical facilities ranged across a wide continuum, but one could readily conclude that ninth graders are well housed. Occasional concern that a building was "cold" (physically and/or psychologically) was expressed, but such judgments were more than offset by notes regarding bright, attractive rooms, clean halls, and growing plants.

3. Students are well behaved and cooperative. Interactions between students and teachers and between the students themselves were courteous, friendly, and open. The decorum of students was apparently better than many expected and it consistently evoked positive comments.

4. Teachers are conscientious, supportive, and well intentioned. Their teaching evidences preparation and planning. Again, observers were quick to point out the readiness of teachers to assist individuals, the businesslike approach taken by teachers, and the professional demeanor they displayed. While the quality of teachers varied considerably, ninth grade teachers are generally able and competent.

5. Students perceive their teachers in a very positive light. They are comfortable with them and see them as helpful and understanding. Certainly, the views of their teachers

expressed by these ninth graders do not reflect the stereotypes often revealed in the media. While students sometimes expressed a negative view of a single teacher, they never spoke disparagingly of all their teachers. The comments made during the interviews about the caring of their teachers and the readiness with which they spoke of particular ones as being understanding were truly heartwarming.

6. Ninth grade students, whether enrolled in a junior high school, a junior-senior high school, or a four-year high school, believe their schools to be excellent. There is, it seems, a strong and almost inherent loyalty to their schools on the part of students.

7. Ninth grade students are generally enrolled in basic academic courses and are not taking an array of "soft" electives. With few exceptions, ninth graders are all taking courses in the areas of language arts, science, mathematics, and social studies. Foreign language, music, physical education, business, home economics, art, health, and industrial arts courses usually round out the day. Computer courses are also frequent.

Generalizations That Identify Areas of Concern

Other images that stand out clearly in the big picture of ninth grade education give rise to some concern. These generalizations point to some of the areas of possible weakness that should enlist the attention of responsible educators.

1. There is a clear lack of meaningful intellectual interaction between students and teachers. All too often student responses were minimal efforts to give the "right" (textbook or previously given) answer. "Discussion" usually meant determining who already knew the answer rather than probing for answers, extending understandings, or relating to local or contemporary affairs. As one analyst phrased it, "the world is reduced to 'true or false' simplicity." There seemed to be little direct concern for, or involvement in, critical thinking or problem solving. Academic expectations appear to be minimal and learning tasks rather routine. This lack of active, decision-making opportunities is contrary to the thrust for autonomy and independence which ninth graders display.

2. The instructional program is heavily dominated by the textbook, and is almost, it seems, restricted by its contents. Relationships between textbook content and the here and now are all too seldom identified. Content is rather cold and canned. It also appears that the great bulk of the ninth grade program is the same irrespective of type of school. While the four-year high schools may offer a greater number of electives the impact on an individual ninth grader's program is limited.

3. The ninth grade program is fragmented into separate subjects. There is almost no curriculum integration or cooperative planning between departments evident. Following a single student inevitably points up this reality in a striking way that surprises teachers and principals who somehow never before realized the tight and artificial separation of life and the world caused by departmentalization.

4. Little provision for diversity exists in the instruction given ninth graders. Activities are almost all of a large group nature with the same expectations and standards applied to the entire group. This too is contrary to the reality of ninth graders as pointed out in Chapter 2.

5. A great deal of class time is taken up in routines—calling roll, distributing papers, waiting. The last 5 or 10 minutes of class is a segment of time that is often little used.

6. Ninth graders are expected to sit for excessive periods of time and to engage in too many passive activities. When educators assume the role of students this reality is revealed dramatically, as the observers discovered.

7. There is an almost complete separation of students' socialization interests and planned classroom activities. The contrast between class time, which seems either to utilize or to

tolerate socialization, and non-class time is sharp. The passivity of ninth grade programs does not correlate well with ninth grader's continuing search for an individual identity.

Recommendations for Program Improvement

Conscientious consideration of the conditions that prevail in ninth grade programs by teachers and administrators can lead to improvement in most of these areas of weakness. Solutions are largely in the hands of the faculties; no outside intervention is essential.

Improvements needed are not dependent upon new state regulations. The basic source of the solution is exactly where the basic problem exists—in the classroom interaction of students and teachers. Because these interactions are complex and involve human beings and human relationships they are not subject to quick fixes, even with money. But they can be improved as professional teachers grapple with their philosophies and methods and institute alterations in their approaches, topics, and procedures.

Some specific points of attack for efforts to improve ninth grade programs follow. It is recognized that these are largely, though not wholly, restatements of the listing of areas of concern noted earlier.

1. Teachers should consider how they can increase the number of *active* activities for ninth graders. The value of hands-on activities is unquestioned, while the amount of sitting is excessive. Efforts expended to correct one will help to correct the other.
2. Teachers should analyze their classroom procedures to determine ways of reducing the time that may be lost in calling role, distributing materials, and waiting on a few students. They should also consider ways to utilize positively those available moments when the major lesson or activity is over but some time remains in the period.
3. The counseling and guidance needs of ninth grade students should be analyzed to see how existing efforts and programs meet these needs. It appears that, currently, students are being shortchanged in this realm, particularly when the ninth grade is located in a high school.

    Since the services of professional counselors are in short supply and likely to remain so, ninth grade teachers should consider ways that they might increase their attention to and support for some of the developmental concerns that ninth graders experience. Schools ought not to assume that ninth graders have "grown up" and only need to be taught the standard subjects. If no schoolwide program dealing with affective education exists, ninth grade teachers should consider ways that they can recognize and meet the needs of their pupils, many of whom are still "in transition."

    A recent survey of teachers in an Ohio public school district pointed up the importance of guidance at the middle level. Teachers were asked to judge whether or not 50 percent or more of their students experienced difficulty in their educational, personal, social, or career adjustment. Nearly 75 percent of the ninth grade teachers judged that their students did not have the motivation and self-discipline to study. In several other items it was clear that ninth grade teachers believed their students need as much guidance as seventh or eighth grade students.
4. Teachers of ninth graders, no matter in what school type they are located, should exert special efforts to increase substantially meaningful intellectual interactions with students. The simple question-and-answer approach which focuses on the *who, where, when,* and *what,* and casts pupils in a passive role needs to be extended to include the *why* and *so what* which challenges students. Most ninth graders now have the mental development that will permit them to think analytically, and they should be assisted in doing so.
5. In 9-12 schools, special provisions should be made to involve ninth graders in student activities. These might include the establishment of activities just for freshmen or

special efforts to recruit ninth graders for those ongoing activities which are, inevitably, run by upper classmen.

6. Intramural programs need to be established for ninth graders who are not "varsity material" but who need and would benefit from involvement in team competition. Few schools of any grade configuration provide the type and variety of physical activities appropriate for their physical and social development.

7. Schools housing ninth graders, particularly 7-12 and 9-12 schools, should institute discussions regarding the needs of ninth graders, the resulting school objectives, and a philosophical context for decision making about both methods and content that reflects these needs and objectives.

Though not directly a conclusion drawn from the shadow study data, the authors believe the ninth grade, especially when it is located in a four-year high school, lacks sufficiently specific and focused objectives, a mission that motivates. These purposes that evolve around the perils of puberty, achieving social and physical maturity, and deciding on one's own personality that underline the early middle grades may have now lost much of their influence and impact. On the other hand, the college preparation and vocational objectives which influence strongly the last years of high school may not yet have come into play.

So the ninth grade, to a degree, is neither "hay nor grass." It exists, to be sure, but it appears to suffer for lack of a strong direction or purpose beyond the academic goals of the individual classes.

For a good many pupils at this level, schooling has lost its appeal. To the below-average pupil, especially, it begins to seem pointless and endless; they have no taste for books. To many who are socially and physically mature but not academically inclined, it seems that school interferes with life rather than school being life. A good many ninth graders become psychological dropouts. Although, lacking any alternative, they may continue to attend physically, their active involvement in gaining an education is minimal and often given begrudgingly.

Nothing in these conclusions constitutes a surprise to educators. The findings of this study of the ninth grade are comparable to those of other studies of schooling reported in the literature in recent years. The findings, for the most part, confirm the often expressed views of those who have studied the process of schooling in action. One is even tempted to go so far as to say that, while the current study was limited to the ninth grade, it probably presents a picture that is representative of upper elementary and secondary education generally.

Where Does the Ninth Grade Belong?

The issue of where the ninth grade belongs is an open question. As is true with the middle level institution (should it be 5-8, 6-8, or 7-9?), there is no right answer. The key lies in the program provided for that grade wherever it is housed. At the same time, it has to be recognized that what is provided and the climate in which it is provided is *inevitably affected by the type of school unit in which it is housed.*

The grade level arrangement selected, from an educational standpoint, may ultimately hinge on the question of who you want to assist and if the presumed benefits for that group offset the inevitable liabilities for another group. Eighth graders may be better off when ninth graders are removed, but ninth graders may be negatively affected in the new environment even though they will experience some pluses. There is always a mixed blessing; for instance, give ninth graders greater access to high school science labs and they are more likely to be tempted by older students to use drugs. An interesting and detailed study of these issues was conducted in one school district by Blyth, Smyth, and Hill (1984).

75

Observers were not asked to express their opinion on the proper placement of the ninth grade, but many did. The most commonly expressed view was supportive of having the ninth grade in the high school. Comments regarding how much more mature ninth graders were than seventh and eighth graders were frequent. On the other hand, there was some implied support for the 7-9 arrangement from observers in such schools. Ninth grade students in high schools during the interviews sometimes expressed their initial apprehension about the size of the school and the difficulties of adjusting—but these had passed by March.

There is no clear-cut educational rationale for organizing schools one way or the other, but there are considerations which must be addressed as the result of any decision made. For instance, if ninth graders are placed in the senior unit, care must be taken to see that they have adequate opportunities for participation in activities and leadership experiences rather than having to wait until they become "upper classmen." Otherwise emerging leadership may become dormant and never reawaken.

By the same token, if the ninth graders are housed in the intermediate unit, provisions will be needed to give eighth graders adequate leadership experiences.

The results of the shadow study project, which focused on the actual classroom experiences of ninth graders, yielded no clear support for either of the two main organizational types. Nor did the comparative analysis aspect, which was specifically designed to measure possible differences, show any advantage. There is simply no inherent educational advantage to any particular form of organization, and educators should not look for or assume any automatic value in one form or another. Since both 7-9 and 9-12 schools exist in large numbers, this conclusion may help educators to focus on the programmatic aspects of the ninth grade which do matter.

A Final Word

The picture of Wednesday, March 7, 1984, as represented by the shadow studies of 141 real ninth graders scattered across the nation, was revealing. It was rich in detail and brought many realities into clear focus. Some of these realities were positive and encouraging; others were negative and disquieting. They all help to set directions for improving the educational experiences of 14 and 15-year-old youngsters, for identifying areas needing further analysis, and for conducting additional research.

The authors hope the project and this written summary will serve as a springboard for getting at the real problems of American education—problems too rarely touched by the kind of recommendations growing out of many of the national studies released in the last few years.

References

Blyth, D. A.; Smyth, C. K.; and Hill, J. P. "Grade Level Arrangements—What Are the Differences?" NASSP Bulletin, April 1984.

Conant, J. B. Recommendations for Education in the Junior High School Years. Princeton, N.J.: Educational Testing Service, 1960.

Gruhn, W. L. "What Do Principals Believe About Grade Organization?" NASSP Bulletin, February 1967.

Lounsbury, J. H., and Marani, J. V. The Junior High School We Saw: One Day in the Eighth Grade. Washington, D.C.: Association for Supervision and Curriculum Development, 1964.

The Shadow Study
Technique

Although the focus of this report is on the findings that emerged from the project, the technique used to gather the data warrants some attention. Shadow studies still are not common, but, when used, they almost always elicit positive comments from those who have experienced the procedure. As adults, we inevitably view schools from adult perceptions. While we consciously seek to serve youth we seem unable to put ourselves in their shoes.

The shadow study technique is an especially effective way of taking off our adult glasses and viewing the school day as youth live it. In addition, it helps us take off the specialist's glasses that we usually wear in observing a subject area teacher.

Many observers in this study, although not asked to react to the procedure, volunteered comments. The following statements are examples.

- "The experience was well worth the time and effort. Every staff member should be afforded this same opportunity to see what school is really like."
- "This was an important opportunity for me as a principal. I am often in classrooms but not for a full day following a student's schedule. It appears different when you do the whole day as a student rather than seeing different teachers."
- "I would recommend that other educators do this. It is an extremely valuable experience . . . try it, you will like and learn from the experience, I can assure you."
- "It was very much of an eye opener for me. It will definitely affect how I do my job and my efforts to personalize what goes on."
- "I feel that more adults should experience what I did today. They might learn more about the students and show a little more compassion."
- "After some 26 years in our school system, it is the first time I have spent a day following a student through his schedule. I found it to be a worthwhile and enlightening experience. It will be recommended that all administrators and department heads should spend a day, either each semester or once a year, shadowing a randomly selected student."
- "What a day! A real education for me."
- "The study helped me by providing a very refreshing insight into an overall school day. . . ."
- "A whole new world opens up when one takes the perspective of the student."

While expressing positive views about the procedure a good many said that the day was tiring. One analyst noted that "over half of the observers reported being extremely tired—both physically (sitting) and mentally."

Observers often expressed sympathy for the students when noting their own fatigue. "I'm tired! It's been a long, full day with only lunch as a break—and that coming at 1:30!" "I was very tired at the end of the day—mostly tired of sitting." "I'm exhausted!"

The shadow study technique has been used occasionally in preservice teacher education. The college student can easily arrange to spend a day in this activity, and it has proven to be a valuable field experience.

Its use with inservice teachers or administrators has been more limited. In part this is due to the fact that relatively few educators are familiar with the technique. In addition, it is difficult to arrange for a teacher or principal to have a full day free of responsibilities.

The technique, however, certainly deserves to be used more frequently. It provides a realistic perspective that cannot be achieved any other way. Too often teachers have no realization of the cumulative effect of the daily schedule on a student. The shadow study provides a means of assessing the impact of the schedule and program on individual pupils.

In addition, by conducting three or four shadow studies within a particular school, data are generated that can be used in curriculum improvement efforts. Often more can be gained by this approach than by the more commonly used technique of sending a few teachers out to visit a "model" school.

The procedure itself is simple. No particular skill or preparation is required. An individual simply shadows a student throughout the school day, making entries relative to what the student is doing every five to seven minutes. Additional columns for noting the environment and making comments are available. A copy of the form used, as well as the directions given observers, are provided below.

While students often figure out before the day is over that they are the ones being followed, there is no indication that this has any significant effect on their behavior or the data gathered.

As an educational tool, this technique merits wider use.

Ninth Grade Study Observation Form

Time	Specific behavior at 5-7 minute intervals	Environment	Impressions-Comments

Directions for Observers

On March 7, 1984, you will be engaging in an important research study. As one of the many volunteer observers from across the country, you will follow a randomly selected ninth grade student and, as nearly as possible, live the school day as he or she does, recording events and impressions. This day will prove to be a valuable, informative, and meaningful experience for you personally. It will also provide the raw data needed to seek an answer to the pertinent question, "How Fares the Ninth Grade?"

To ensure reasonable objectivity, uniformity, and success, please read the following directions and follow them carefully.

1. Make prior arrangements with the school to be visited if other than your own. It is important that teachers understand the purpose of your visit and know that you are *not* evaluating them or the school.

2. Clear your calendar for March 7 so that you will be free the entire day to complete the shadow study.

3. Arrive at the school 15 minutes or so ahead of the school opening. Secure, or arrange for securing, the basic data called for on the cover sheet provided.

4. Select a ninth grade student using a technique, such as one of the following, that will ensure randomness:

    (a) Ask someone to pick a number between 1 and 25. On the roster of ninth grade students whose last name starts with your middle initial, select that numbered student.

    (b) Locate the file drawer of ninth grade student folders and pick, blindly, a folder. (Note: if the student selected is in a special education class for more than 25 percent of the day, pick another student.)

5. Locate the selected student's homeroom (or first period) and, with the help of the teacher, identify unobtrusively the student to be shadowed. Find a seat out of the way and look as nonchalant as possible.

6. Using the forms provided, record the information desired. While you can't be oblivious to other matters, try to keep your focus on the individual student and what he or she is apparently doing. (Use initial or fictitious name for student shadowed.)

7. The five to seven-minute time interval will give you a bit of flexibility, but will definitely show the flow of actions and activities.

    Start a new time interval with each change of class or period. Go with the student to gym, lunch, and, as nearly as possible, keep up with the individual so you can experience vicariously his or her full school day.

8. If the student, after the third or fourth period, confronts you with the question, "Are you following me?" pass it with a counter question such as, "You know, I guess you have been in every class I've visited." In this and all cases, your intuition and common sense will be the best guide.

9. At the close of the last period (or close to it if you've cleared with teacher), pull the student aside for an interview. (See separate sheet for details on interview and list of questions.) You may want to tape record the interview.

10. If you are not in your school, check out with the office, secure additional information needed, and express appreciation.

11. That evening, if at all possible, write out your impressions, reactions, and conclusions while the day's events are still fresh in your mind.

12. Mail the complete study, the interview, the general data sheet, and your personal reflections to NASSP.

Observers Who Conducted Shadow Studies

WILLIAM M. ALEXANDER
University of Florida
Gainesville, Fla.

HELEN ANDREWS
Elma HS
Elma, Wash.

JACQUELINE M. ANGLIN
University of Akron
Akron, Ohio

GEORGE M. ARNOLD
Owensville JrHS
Owensville, Mo.

ROLLAN AUBERT
Wood River Rural Jr/Sr HS
Wood River, Nebr.

GENE BALINT
Cascade MS
Longview, Wash.

MYRNA H. BARKER
Sequatchie County Board of Education
Dunlap, Tenn.

GEORGIA BARNWELL
Five Forks MS
Lawrenceville, Ga.

EMMA BASS
Annie Camp JrHS
Jonesboro, Ark.

ARTHUR A. BIEDERMAN
Twality JrHS
Tigard, Oreg.

JOAN M. BLOOMER
Culpeper HS
Culpeper, Va.

SHIRLEY BOBO
Milwood Jr/Sr HS
Oklahoma City, Okla.

GARY BRAGER
Baltimore County Public Schools
Towson, Md.

EDWARD G. BRANISH
Towanda SrHS
Towanda, Pa.

WARREN M. BREWER
Horace Mann MS
Sheboygan, Wis.

ESTELLE BRUNETTI
John Glenn HS
Norwalk, Calif.

STANLEY O. CAREY
Niles West HS
Skokie, Ill.

LARRY CARLSON
Woodbrook JrHS
Tacoma, Wash.

IVAN W. CENDESE
Glendale Intermediate School
NE Salt Lake City, Utah

MARTIN CHORBA
Timberline HS
Lacy, Wash.

ROBERT CHRISTENSON
George Washington JrHS
Ridgewood, N.J.

FAITH M. CLEARY
John Philip Sousa JrHS
Port Washington, N.Y.

PAULINE CLINE
Edmonds HS
Edmonds, Wash.

GWENDOLYN J. COOKE
William H. Lemell MS
Baltimore, Md.

RICHARD J. CORMIER
Van Buren District
Secondary School
Van Buren, Maine

PETER CORRODI
Middleville JrHS
Northport, N.Y.

JAMES R. "PETE" CROWLEY
Hermosa JrHS
Farmington, N.Mex.

LOU ANN DALDRUP
Sabino HS
Tucson, Ariz.

BONNIE DANIELS
Glenelg HS
Glenelg, Md.

HAL ELLIS
Mount Vernon HS
Mount Vernon, Wash.

BRUCE EMBERSON
South JrHS
Eau Clair, Wis.

CECIL L. FLYNN
Wellington-Napoleon R-9
Wellington, Mo.

DAVID M. GAILEY
Greeley County HS
Tribune, Kans.

ROBERTA GLASER
Deer Park HS
Cincinnati, Ohio

HARRY GOLDBERG
Clark Lane JrHS
Waterford, Conn.

BILL HAFFEY
Arbor Heights JrHS
Omaha, Nebr.

PHIL HARRED
Elgin Jr/Sr HS
Elgin, Okla.

CAROL HARRINGTON
Bethel HS
Bethel, Conn.

EDWARD HARRINGTON
Williams Area HS
Williamsport, Pa.

BOB HARTMAN
Howard HS
Ellicott City, Md.

HOWARD HASKEN
West HS
Anchorage, Alaska

DEAN A. HAUGEN
Hunt JrHS
Tacoma, Wash.

CHARLES M. HENRY
Wheaton-Warrenville MS
Wheaton, Ill.

KARLEY HIGGINS
Staples HS
Westport, Conn.

LOUIS L. HIGGINS
Oxford HS
Oxford, Ala.

DEAN HOUGHTON
Mill River Union HS
North Clarendon, Vt.

GENE HUFF
Oakland JrHS
Columbia, Mo.

J. CASEY HURLEY
Stoughton HS
Stoughton, Wis.

BILLIE JAMES
Lincoln JrHS
Cottage Grove, Oreg.

CHRISTINE JENSEN
Kodiak JrHS
Kodiak, Alaska

JEANNE L. JOHNSON
Lynnwood HS
Lynnwood, Wash.

J. HOWARD JOHNSTON
University of Cincinnati
Cincinnati, Ohio

FLORA JOY
East Tennessee State University
Johnson City, Tenn.

DAN KAHLER
Oak Park HS
Kansas City, Mo.

STEVE KAISER
Connersville HS
Connersville, Tenn.

RONALD KELLEY
Western Hills JrHS
Cranston, R.I.

DOROTHE M. KRAYER
North Shore HS
West Palm Beach, Fla.

KENNETH LARGESS
Shrewsbury HS
Shrewsbury, Mass.

ANTHONY LAROSA
Melrose JrHS
Melrose, Mass.

LEWIS LARRISON
Parkview JrHS
New Castle, Ind.

EARL LEBAKKEN
West Bend HS
West Bend, Wis.

ANDREAS P. LEHNER
Harwood Union HS
Moretown, Vt.

LOWELL C. LENARZ
Oskaloosa JrHS
Oskaloosa, Iowa

ROSE LEVINE
Wilde Lake HS
Columbia, Md.

H. WAYNE LINTON
Blevins JrHS
Fort Collins, Colo.

BARBARA J. LITTLE
Eagle Valley JrHS
Carson City, Nev.

KENNETH M. LONG
Norristown Area HS
Norristown, Pa.

JOHN H. LOUNSBURY
Georgia College
Milledgeville, Ga.

CHERIE MAJOR-FOSTER
University of Maine
Gorham, Maine

RENE MALMGREN
Aurora Central HS
Aurora, Colo.

GARY MANNING
University of Alabama-Birmingham
Birmingham, Ala.

JACK MARTIN
East Washington University
Cheney, Wash.

WILLIAM B. MARTIN
East Carolina University
Greenville, N.C.

ERNESTA MASAGATANI
Stevenson Intermediate School
Honolulu, Hawaii

REGINALD MCDONALD
Portland HS
Portland, Maine

LEE MCFADDEN
Henderson HS
Westchester, Pa.

LOUISE MCLAUGHLIN
Atholton HS
Columbia, Md.

CAROLE MCWILLIAM
Hawthorne JrHS
Pocatello, Idaho

PAT MEEKS
Hot Springs HS
Truth or Consequences, N.Mex.

ROBERT C. MEERDINK
Patricia Henry JrHS
Sioux Falls, S.Dak.

ELLIOT Y. MERENBLOOM
Pikesville MS
Baltimore, Md.

RONALD I. MONTGOMERY
Yelm HS
Yelm, Wash.

AMY W. MOOK
Minnetonka HS
Minnetonka, Minn.

FRANK J. MOTTA
River View HS
Kennewick, Wash.

EDWIN A. MURBACH
Sylvania Southview HS
Sylvania, Ohio

LINDA H. MYERS
Evart HS
Evart, Mich.

LYNNE NEELEY
R.A. Long HS
Longview, Wash.

TOM NELSON
Stewart JrHS
Tacoma, Wash.

ELLY NIELSEN
University HS
University of Hawaii
Honolulu, Hawaii

ALLAN OLCHOWSKI
Mt. Hebron HS
Ellicott City, Md.

LYNN OLDACKER
University of Florida
Gainesville, Fla.

STEPHEN K. O'NEIL
Bow Memorial HS
Bow, N.H.

DOUGLAS OTJEN
Meeker JrHS
Tacoma, Wash.

VERNON PAULS
McPherson JrHS
McPherson, Kans.

ROBERT J. PETERSON
Cudahy JrHS
Cudahy, Wis.

JOSEPH PETRELLA
Pablo Casals Intermediate School
Bronx, N.Y.

FRED PFLUGRATH
Columbia HS
Hunters, Wash.

ROBERT J. PLAIA
Memorial JrHS
Huntington Station, N.Y.

KATHERYN POWELL
Georgia College
Milledgeville, Ga.

R. JAMES PRATT
Bedford HS
Bedford, Pa.

GEORGE W. PUGH
North Kitsap HS
Poulsbo, Wash.

JAMES C. QUEEN
H.D. Woodson HS
Washington, D.C.

EDWARD J. RAK
Shaler Area Intermediate School
Glenshaw, Pa.

DENNIS RETTKE
Morris MS
Morris, Minn.

STANLEY ROBINSON
Lynnfield HS
Lynnfield, Mass.

ROGER H. ROUSSELLE
Attleboro HS
Attleboro, Mass.

JOHN SACKMAN
Encampment Jr/Sr HS
Encampment, Wyo.

ARTHUR SALAZAR
Espanola JrHS
Espanola, N.Mex.

ROBERT J. SAUTER
Deer Valley HS
Phoenix, Ariz.

AL SCHMITH
A.G. Huldtloff JrHS
Tacoma, Wash.

MELVIN SCHNAUER
Richland HS
Richland, Wash.

RODNEY SCHOTT
Tumwater HS
Tumwater, Wash.

KENNETH SCHULTZ
Hampton HS
Allison Park, Pa.

JANET S. SELAVKA
Wheeler HS
North Stonington, Conn.

BESS SHEA
Centennial HS
Ellicott City, Md.

GERALYN SHREVE
Shorline HS
Seattle, Wash.

RONALD SILLS
Mt. Blue JrHS
Farmington, Maine

O. WRAY SMITH
Paul Dorman HS
Spartanburg, S.C.

BARBARA A. SOUTHALL
Triton Regional School
Byfield, Mass.

ROBERT SPERRIT
Bronxville Jr/Sr HS
Bronxville, N.Y.

ROBERT ST. CLAIR
Hopkins West JrHS
Minnetonka, Minn.

LOIS STIEGEMEIER
St. Charles West HS
St. Charles, Mo.

CHARLES A. STOLSIG
Winston Churchill HS
Eugene, Oreg.

GENE STREAGLE
Oakland Mills HS
Columbia, Md.

ANTHONY J. STRUZZIERO
Belmonte Saugus JrHS
Saugus, Mass.

JAN SWARTZ
Cashman JrHS
Las Vegas, Nev.

NORMA LEE TAYLOR
John Adams JrHS
Charleston, W.Va.

LYLE W. TOBIN
Canby HS
Canby, Minn.

ROGER L. TUCKER
Highland HS
Salt Lake City, Utah

THURMAN WAITS
Pepperell MS
Lindale, Ga.

RAMONA WARD
East Central HS
San Antonio, Tex.

DAVID WASHBURN
Urbana JrHS
Urbana, Ill.

GLORIA WASHINGTON
Hammond HS
Columbia, Md.

ROBERT C. WHILE
Twin Spruce JrHS
Gillette, Wyo.

BETTY LOU WHITFORD
University of Louisville
Louisville, Ky.

DALE W. WILLARD
Five Forks MS
Lawrenceville, Ga.

JOHN YONKER
Hughes JrHS
Bismarck, N. Dak.

Schools in Which
Observations Took Place

JOHN ADAMS JrHS
Charleston, W.Va.

ARBOR HEIGHTS JrHS
Omaha, Nebr.

ATHOLTON HS
Columbia, Md.

ATTLEBORO HS
Attleboro, Mass.

AURORA CENTRAL HS
Aurora, Colo.

E.B. AYCOCK JrHS
Greenville, N.C.

BEDFORD AREA HS
Bedford, Pa.

BELMONTE SAUGUS JrHS
Saugus, Mass.

BETHEL HS
Bethel, Conn.

BLEVINS JrHS
Ft. Collins, Colo.

BODDIE JrHS
Milledgeville, Ga.

BOW MEMORIAL SCHOOL
Bow, N.H.

BRONXVILLE Jr/Sr HS
Bronxville, N.Y.

BROOKWOOD HS
Snellville, Ga.

BROOKWOOD HS
Lawrenceville, Ga.

BROWN SCHOOL
Louisville, Ky.

CANBY HS
Canby, Minn.

CASHMAN JrHS
Las Vegas, Nev.

CASTLE HILL JrHS 127
Bronx, N.Y.

CENTENNIAL HS
Ellicott City, Md.

COLUMBIA HS
Hunters, Wash.

CONNERSVILLE HS
Connersville, Ind.

CUDAHY HS EAST
Cudahy, Wis.

CULPEPER COUNTY JrHS
Culpeper, Va.

CUYAHOGA FALLS HS
Cuyahoga, Ohio

DEER PARK JrHS
Randallstown, Md.

DEER PARK HS
Cincinnati, Ohio

DEER VALLEY HS
Glendale, Ariz.

PAUL M. DORMAN HS
Spartanburg, S.C.

DULANEY HS
Timonium, Md.

85

EAGLE VALLEY JrHS
Carson City, Nev.

EAST CENTRAL HS
San Antonio, Tex.

EDMONDS HS
Edmonds, Wash.

T.J. ELDER JrHS
Sandersville, Ga.

ELGIN Jr/Sr HS
Elgin, Okla.

ELMA HS
Elma, Wash.

ENCAMPMENT Jr/Sr HS
Encampment, Wyo.

ESPANOLA VALLEY HS
Espanola, N.Mex.

EVART Jr/Sr HS
Evart, Mich.

FOWLER JrHS
Tigard, Oreg.

GAINESVILLE HS
Gainesville, Fla.

GLENELG HS
Glenelg, Md.

JOHN GLENN HS
Norwalk, Calif.

GREELEY COUNTY HS
Tribune, Kans.

GREENACRES JrHS
Greenacres, Wash.

HAMMOND HS
Columbia, Md.

HAMPTON HS
Allison Park, Pa.

HARWOOD UNION HS
Moretown, Vt.

HAWTHORNE JrHS
Pocatello, Idaho

HENDERSON HS
West Chester, Pa.

HERMOSA JrHS
Farmington, N.Mex.

HIGHLAND HS
Salt Lake City, Utah

HOT SPRINGS HS
Truth or Consequences, N. Mex.

HOWARD HS
Ellicott City, Md.

HUDTLOFF JrHS
Tacoma, Wash.

HUGHES JrHS
Bismarck, N.Dak.

H.F. HUNT JrHS
Tacoma, Wash.

KODIAK HS
Kodiak, Alaska

WILLIAM H. LEMMEL MS
Baltimore, Md.

LINCOLN JrHS
Cottage Grove, Oreg.

R.A. LONG HS
Longview, Wash.

LYNNFIELD HS
Lynnfield, Mass.

LYNNWOOD HS
Lynnwood, Wash.

MARK MORRIS HS
Longview, Wash.

MCPHERSON JrHS
McPherson, Kans.

MEEKER JrHS
Tacoma, Wash.

MELROSE JrHS
Melrose, Mass.

MEMORIAL JrHS
Huntington Station, N.Y.

MIDDLEVILLE JrHS
Northport, N.Y.

MIDFIELD HS
Midfield, Ala.

MILL RIVER UNION HS
North Clarendon, Vt.

MILLWOOD Jr/Sr HS
Oklahoma City, Okla.

MINNETONKA HS
Minnetonka, Minn.

MORRIS SrHS
Morris, Minn.

MT. ARARAT SCHOOL
Topsham, Maine

MT. BLUE JrHS
Farmington, Maine

MT. HEBRON HS
Ellicott City, Md.

MT. VERNON HS
Mt. Vernon, Wash.

NILES WEST HS
Skokie, Ill.

NORRISTOWN AREA HS
Norristown, Pa.

NORTH HS
Sheboygan, Wis.

NORTH KITSAP HS
Poulsbo, Wash.

NORTH SHORE COMMUNITY HS
West Palm Beach, Fla.

OAKLAND JrHS
Columbia, Mo.

OAKLAND MILLS HS
Columbia, Md.

OAK PARK HS
Kansas City, Mo.

OSKALOOSA JrHS
Oskaloosa, Iowa

OWENSVILLE JrHS
Owensville, Mo.

OXFORD HS
Oxford, Ala.

PARKVIEW JrHS
New Castle, Ind.

PATRICK HENRY JrHS
Sioux Falls, S.Dak.

PEPPERELL HS
Lindale, Ga.

PORTLAND HS
Portland, Maine

RICHLAND HS
Richland, Wash.

RIVER VIEW HS
Kennewick, Wash.

SABINO HS
Tucson, Ariz.

ST. CHARLES WEST SrHS
St. Charles, Mo.

ST. LOUIS PARK SrHS
St. Louis Park, Minn.

SANTA FE HS
Alachua, Fla.

SEQUATCHIE COUNTY HS
Dunlap, Tenn.

SHALER AREA INTERMEDIATE
SCHOOL
Glenshaw, Pa.

SHORELINE HS
Seattle, Wash.

SHREWSBURY HS
Shrewsbury, Mass.

JOHN PHILIP SOUSA JrHS
Port Washington, N.Y.

SOUTH AMHERST HS
South Amherst, Ohio

SOUTH JrHS
Eau Claire, Wis.

STAPLES HS
Westport, Conn.

R.L. STEVENSON INTERMEDIATE
SCHOOL
Honolulu, Hawaii

STEWART JrHS
Tacoma, Wash.

STOUGHTON HS
Stoughton, Wis.

SYLVANIA SOUTHVIEW HS
Sylvania, Ohio

TIMBERLINE HS
Lacey, Wash.

TOLLAND HS
Tolland, Conn.

TOWANDA SrHS
Towanda, Pa.

TRITON REGIONAL SCHOOL
Byfield, Mass.

TWIN SPRUCE JrHS
Gillette, Wyo.

TUMWATER HS
Tumwater, Wash.

UNIVERSITY HS
Honolulu, Hawaii

UNIVERSITY SCHOOL
Johnson City, Tenn.

URBANA JrHS
Urbana, Ill.

VAN BUREN SECONDARY SCHOOL
Van Buren, Maine

GEORGE WASHINGTON JrHS
Ridgewood, N.J.

WATERFORD HS
Waterford, Conn.

WELLINGTON-NAPOLEON R-9
Wellington, Mo.

WEST HS
Salt Lake City, Utah

WEST ANCHORAGE HS
Anchorage, Alaska

WEST BEND WEST HS
West Bend, Wis.

WESTERN HILLS JrHS
Cranston, R.I.

WESTSIDE HS
Jonesboro, Ark.

WHEATON CENTRAL HS
Wheaton, Ill.

WHEELER Jr/Sr HS
Stonington, Conn.

WILDE LAKE HS
Columbia, Md.

WILLIAMSPORT AREA HS
Williamsport, Pa.

WINSTON CHURCHILL HS
Eugene, Oreg.

WOOD RIVER RURAL Jr/Sr HS
Wood River, Nebr.

WOODBROOK JrHS
Tacoma, Wash.

H.D. WOODSON HS
Washington, D.C.

YELM HS
Yelm, Wash.

APPENDIX   D

General Analysts

Edward A. Barnhart
  Principal, Sterling MS
  East Wenatchee, Wash.

Emma Lee Bass
  Principal, Annie Camp MS
  Jonesboro, Ark.

Joan M. Bloomer
  Principal, Culpeper County JrHS
  Culpeper, Va

Warren Brewer
  Principal, Horace Mann MS
  Sheboygan, Wis.

Joan Delaney
  Principal, Parker JrHS
  Reading, Mass.

Tom Erb
  Associate Professor, University of Kansas
  Lawrence, Kans.

Raymond Flaherty
  Teacher, Hampstead MS
  Hampstead, N.H.

Larry Holt
  Assistant Professor, University of
    Wisconsin
  Platteville, Wis.

Don Havland
  Assistant Superintendent, Stillwater
    Public Schools
  Stillwater, Minn.

Lewis Larrison
  Principal, Parkview JrHS
  New Castle, Ind.

Robert E. Lowery
  Professor, Seattle University
  Seattle, Wash.

Kenneth McEwin
  Professor, Appalachian State University
  Boone, N.C.

Dan Michaels
  Teacher, Owen Brown MS
  Columbia, Md.

Joseph Petrella
  Principal, Intermediate School 181X
  Bronx, N.Y.

Velma Pitcher
  Teacher, Bloomington JrHS
  Bloomington, Ill.

Cynthia Rutherford
  Teacher
  Wichita, Kans.

Ann Shelley
  Professor, Bethany College
  Bethany, W.Va.

Katie Sheppard
  Teacher, Boddie JrHS
  Milledgeville, Ga.

Geralyn Shreve
  Teacher, Shoreline HS
  Seattle, Wash.

David Strahan
  Assistant Professor, University of North
    Carolina
  Greensboro, N.C.

Frank Yulo
  Professor, South Connecticut State
    University
  New Haven, Conn.

Guidelines for Analysts

To assist you in carrying out your analysis of the enclosed shadow studies, the following guidelines are provided. They will also help to ensure a reasonable degree of commonality in coverage and assist in further analysis.

The analysis should be done in two parts—one essentially summarizing what observers tell us about ninth grade programs, and one in which you draw conclusions and make your personal judgments.

We suggest you read the studies through once simply to get a sense for them. Then go through them making notes about such matters as the 12 questions listed in Part I below. You may or may not seek to answer each of these questions specifically, but do try to cover these topics as well as others that occur to you, to summarize the reality of ninth grade programs. Note examples, include direct quotations or paraphrased statements.

Parts II and III should be completed in the spaces provided, if possible.

After you have completed your analysis, please return it and the studies themselves to NASSP by June 22.

I. *What Did Observers Tell Us About These Ninth Graders?*
1. How were the students grouped during the day? On what basis?
2. What kind of social encounters did the students have during the day?
3. In what skill areas did the students receive *direct* instruction and how much time was spent on this skill instruction?
4. To whom did the students talk? Under what circumstances?
5. Who talked to the students during the day? Under what circumstances?
6. Were students provided with a chance to explore new topics or subjects? What were some of these exploratory activities? How were these opportunities provided: in the regular curriculum, or by special courses or programs?
7. To what extent was the content studied during the day related to student interests, the current state of knowledge in the subject area, and the world outside of school?
8. What kinds of instructional models and approaches seemed to predominate?
9. What kinds of physical surroundings seemed to predominate? How were classes arranged?
10. How did school time seem to be spent?
11. Describe the school climates that seemed to predominate.
12. What kind of physical activity did the students engage in?

II. *Conclusions That You Draw from Reading These Studies*

Based on the information in the reports, draw two or three conclusions about each topic or area listed below. Place an asterisk (*) next to any of those about which you are especially certain. Place a question mark (?) next to any about which you have some doubts.

A. Curriculum Content (subject matter)

90   B. Teaching Arrangements (departmentalized, team teaching, block scheduling)

C. Instruction and Teaching Methods

D. Teacher-Student Interaction

E. Student-Student Interaction

F. Physical Environment

G. Advising and Counseling

H. Opportunities for Social Skill Learning

I. Teacher and Student Use of Class Time

J. School Learning Climate (student and teacher attitudes)

III. After reflecting on the reports you have read, your reactions to them, and the comments of the site visitors, please report any other conclusions or observations that you believe are relevant to this study of ninth grade programs.

Comparative Analysts

Sherrel Bergmann
National College of Education
Evanston, Ill.

Mary Downey Bracegirdle
Cobb County Public Schools
Marietta, Ga.

Bruce Brombacher
Jones JrHS
Upper Arlington, Ohio

Terry Brooks
Highland MS
Louisville, Ky.

Anne Marie Collins
McCarty MS
Gresham, Oreg.

Mary Compton
University of Georgia
Athens, Ga.

Tim Daniels
Upper Darby School District
Upper Darby, Pa.

Donald Eichhorn
Lewisburg Area School District
Lewisburg, Pa.

Carol Fillenberg
Westminster Schools District #50
Westminster, Colo.

Lucille Freeman
East Central University
Ada, Okla.

James Garvin
Gordon College
Wenham, Mass.

Joan Grady
Horizon MS
Aurora, Colo.

Linda Hopping
Holcomb Bridge MS
Alpharetta, Ga.

Ron Johnson
L'Anse Creuse MS
Mount Clemons, Mich.

Laural Kanthak
Susanne Intermediate School
Walnut, Calif.

Edward Lawton
College of Charleston
Charleston, S.C.

Burma Lockridge
Fulton County Schools
Atlanta, Ga.

Cherie Major-Foster
University of Maine
Gorham, Maine

Larry Pigg
Laramie JrHS
Laramie, Wyo.

Ronald Rolph
Birmingham Public School District
Birmingham, Mich.

Robert St. Clair
  Hopkins West JrHS
  Minnetonka, Minn.

Georgann Seekings
  Woodbury JrHS
  Shaker Heights, Ohio

Gordon Vars
  Kent State University
  Kent, Ohio

David Washburn
  Urbana JrHS
  Urbana, Ill.

Directions for Comparative Evaluation of Ninth Grade Shadow Studies

The questions on the checksheet relate to conditions that many see as proper or desirable ones for ninth grade programs. Though it is not expected that evidence on all of them would be present in a single day's schooling, the list does provide a somewhat objective basis for rating the general effectiveness of programs. The study is not rating individual schools. It seeks to compare the programs provided for ninth graders in the terminal grade of an intermediate unit, in the entry grade of a high school, and in a middle grade of a junior/senior high school.

Please review individually the small group, randomly selected shadow studies, *completing a checksheet for each study.* (Be sure that you fill in *the correct code number for each sheet.*) Please return the studies and the checksheets by _____ .

Your assistance in this important phase of the ninth grade project is greatly appreciated.